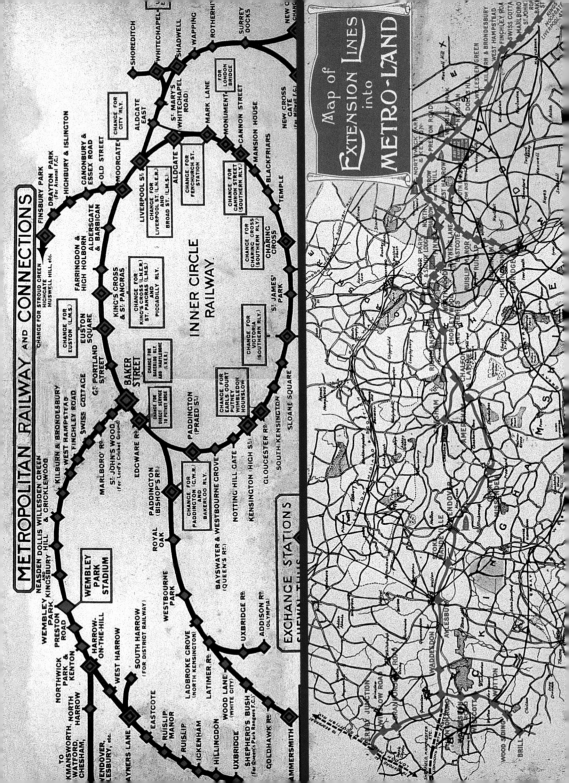

METROPOLITAN RAILWAY and CONNECTIONS

Map of EXTENSION LINES into METRO-LAND

INNER CIRCLE RAILWAY.

EXCHANGE STATIONS

WEMBLEY PARK STADIUM

Stations referenced include:

FINSBURY PARK (For Arsenal F.C.)
DRAYTON PARK
CHANGE FOR STROUD GREEN HIGHGATE MUSWELL HILL etc.
SHOREDITCH
WHITECHAPEL
SHADWELL
WAPPING
ROTHERHITHE
SURREY DOCKS
NEW CROSS
NEW CROSS GATE (For Mill Hill, etc.)
ALDGATE EAST
ST. MARY'S (WHITECHAPEL ROAD)
MARK LANE
FOR LONDON BRIDGE
MONUMENT
CANNON STREET
MANSION HOUSE
BLACKFRIARS
TEMPLE
CHANGE FOR CANNON STREET (SOUTHERN RLY.)
CHARING CROSS
CHANGE FOR CHARING CROSS (SOUTHERN RLY.)
ST. JAMES' PARK
CHANGE FOR VICTORIA (SOUTHERN RLY.)
SLOANE SQUARE
SOUTH KENSINGTON
GLOUCESTER RD.
KENSINGTON (HIGH ST.)
NOTTING HILL GATE
CHANGE FOR EARLS COURT PUTNEY WIMBLEDON HOUNSLOW
ALDGATE
CHANGE FOR LIVERPOOL ST. (L.N.E.R.) AND BROAD ST. (L.M.S.)
ST. MARY'S
CHANGE FOR FENCHURCH ST. STATION
LIVERPOOL ST.
MOORGATE
CANONBURY & ESSEX ROAD
HIGHBURY & ISLINGTON
OLD STREET
CHANGE FOR CITY RLY.
ALDERSGATE & BARBICAN
FARRINGDON & HIGH HOLBORN
KING'S CROSS & ST. PANCRAS
CHANGE FOR KING'S CROSS (L.N.E.R.) ST. PANCRAS (L.M.S.) AND PICCADILLY RLY.
EUSTON SQUARE
CHANGE FOR EUSTON (L.M.S.)
GT. PORTLAND STREET
BAKER STREET
CHANGE FOR BAKERLOO RLY. AND MARYLEBONE (L.N.E.R.)
MARLBORO' RD.
ST. JOHN'S WOOD (For Lord's Cricket Ground)
EDGWARE RD.
PADDINGTON (PRAED ST.)
CHANGE FOR DIRECT SERVICE TO PUTNEY BRIDGE
SWISS COTTAGE
FINCHLEY ROAD
WEST HAMPSTEAD
KILBURN & BRONDESBURY
WILLESDEN GREEN
DOLLIS HILL & CRICKLEWOOD
NEASDEN
WEMBLEY PARK
PRESTON ROAD
KINGSBURY
NORTHWICK PARK & KENTON
TO WATFORD, CHESHAM, WENDOVER, AYLESBURY, etc.
KINASWORTH
HARROW-ON-THE-HILL
WEST HARROW
SOUTH HARROW (For District Railway)
RAYNERS LANE
EASTCOTE
RUISLIP MANOR
RUISLIP
ICKENHAM
HILLINGDON
UXBRIDGE
PADDINGTON (BISHOP'S RD.)
ROYAL OAK
WESTBOURNE PARK
CHANGE FOR PADDINGTON (G.W.R.) AND BAKERLOO RLY.
LADBROKE GROVE (NORTH KENSINGTON)
LATIMER RD.
WOOD LANE (WHITE CITY)
SHEPHERD'S BUSH (For Queen's Park Rangers F.C.)
GOLDHAWK RD.
HAMMERSMITH
BAYSWATER & WESTBOURNE GROVE
UXBRIDGE RD.
ADDISON RD. (OLYMPIA)

List of Colour Illustrations

Front cover: A wintry day at Pinner in the heart of Metro-land, in 1924 before electrification. The Met H class 4-4-4T heads a rake of Dreadnought coaches and a Pullman car that left Verney Junction at 09.26 and is due at Liverpool Street at 10.40. *(Peter Green)*

Page 2, top: Looking west at Baker Street station soon after the opening in 1863, with gas lighting to augment the daylight filtering down through the shafts on either side. It shows clearly the mixed gauge tracks for the Met and GWR. *(Chromolith by S Hodson)*

Page 2, bottom: The Great Central Railway began to share the Met tracks in 1899 and here, a lightly-loaded Manchester bound express, headed by a Robinson class 8 4-6-0 engine, is about to pass Rickmansworth. *(John Quick/ GCRS)*

Page 3, top: Neasden Engine shed was the base for Met locomotives. Here, a venerable Beyer-Peacock class A 4-4-0T, as L45 in 1938, and now fitted with a cab to protect the crew, rests in front of the cooling towers of the Met power station. *(Colour-Rail LT1)*

Page 3, bottom: The interior of a 'Ladies Only' compartment in an Ashbury coach, originally built around 1890 as steam-hauled stock, then converted to electric traction and later pressed into service for the Chesham 'Shuttle' from 1941 to 1961.*(Clive Foxell)*

Page 4: Met carriage maps of the Inner Circle and Extension routes. *(Clive Foxell)*

Pages 72-75: Metro-land publicity. *(Clive Foxell)*

Page 165, top: Examples of Met T stock multiple electric units at the southern end of Harrow-on- the-Hill station in 1951. The nearer train is a fast Aldgate and the other a stopping all-stations Baker Street. *(Dewi Williams)*

Page 165 bottom: Whilst the 1980s saw the supremacy of the BR diesel multiple units on the routes from Marylebone, as shown here, steam specials became popular. Ex-SR 4-6-0 no.777 'Sir Lamiel' heads a train from Marylebone bound for Stratford.*(Clive Foxell)*

Page 166 top: Although it was too late to influence matters, English Electric privately developed GT3, a stylish gas turbine locomotive with a familiar outline. With express disc codes, it passes Moor Park bound for Marylebone in 1961. *(Colour-Rail DE 2025)*

Page 166 bottom: November 1965, the end of steam is nigh, and by this time the old Great Central Railway line was in the hands of BR Midland Region. A tired Britannia 4-6-0, 'Vulcan' from Nottingham, heads past LT electric A60 stock at Northwick Park. *(Colour-Rail BRE1668)*

Page167 top: The Chiltern Railways depot at Aylesbury in 2005, with their class 168 and 170 diesel turbo cars either side of a heritage DU being refurbished for route training purposes. *(Clive Foxell)*

Page 167, bottom: An illustration of the new multiple-electric stock ordered by Metronet for use on the Met and expected to come into use from 2009. *(Bombardier)*

Rear cover: The classic brass interior door handle used in Met carriages, carrying the splendid exhortation – *'LIVE IN METRO-LAND'*. *(Clive Foxell)*

to my dear wife Shirley, for her support and encouragement

First Published 2005

By Clive Foxell at: 4 Meades Lane, Chesham, Bucks, HP5 1ND

Railway histories also by the author:
Chesham Shuttle (1996)
Chesham Branch Album (1998)
The Met & GC Joint Line trilogy –
Story of the Met & GC Joint Line (2000)
Memories of the Met & GC Joint Line (2002)
Rails to Metro-land (2005)

ISBN 0 9529184 5 5

Printed by: Stanley Mason Printers Ltd.,
61 Woodside Road
Amersham, Bucks, HP6 6AA

Rails to METRO-LAND

Dr Clive Foxell CBE FREng

*"I know a land where the wild flowers grow,
Near, near at hand if by train you go,
Metro-land, Metro-land,
Meadows sweet have a golden glow,
Hills are green as the vales below,
In Metro-land, Metro-land"*

George Robert Sims (1847-1922),
  – possibly the first mention of the word Metro-land

PREFACE

A century ago, the Metropolitan Railway had been extended from a profitable base in central London to the sparsely populated countryside to the north-west of Buckinghamshire by Sir Edward Watkin, a contentious Victorian entrepreneur. This push through the Chilterns was part of his ambitious scheme to link Manchester by rail to Paris. Although Watkin's plans failed with his death, a number of the untoward consequences of his actions fortuitously put his successors at the 'Met' in an unique position to exploit the surplus land adjacent to their lines, under the banner of 'Metro-land'.

This seminal campaign created the image of an idealistic post-war lifestyle, based upon the concept of affordable housing of an individualistic character, set in pleasant countryside and yet within easy reach of London by the 'Met'. The propagation of the 'Metro-land' brand led to its wide adoption by the media and incorporation into our culture as epitomising a way of life. Indeed, it was so successful that the Met had to embark on a continuing programme of improving capacity to match the resulting growth in commuting.

Part of the attraction of Metro-land has always been the charming character of its trains. Again, this is largely due to Watkin having built the 'last main line', in the shape of the Great Central Railway (GCR), from the north to join the Met in Bucks and thence to a new terminus at Marylebone. However, with the end of his dream, a joint company had to be formed to manage this part, under rules of fiendish complexity. Even today, the rails to Metro-land remain as a 'Joint' operation between London Transport (LT) and Chiltern Railways.

I have been privileged to be a Metro-lander for most of my life: being born in Harrow, going to school near the line and able to watch the ebbing influence of the Met and the GCR, acting as a cleaner at Neasden Loco Shed, undertaking an apprenticeship at Wembley and lastly, commuting by train from Chesham. I hope that this book will explain the origins, construction and evolution of such a varied and fascinating railway and also the nature of Metro-land, which has become part of our heritage.

Clive Foxell
Autumn 2005, Chesham

ACKNOWLEDGEMENTS

Key ingredients of this book are the illustrations. Although it has become progressively more difficult to illustrate this series with fresh material as more historical railway books are published and smaller existing private photographic collections are dispersed, I have been fortunate in finding pictures that I hope will be mainly unfamiliar to readers. Such treasures often come from individuals and here I wish to thank most sincerely Robert Barker, Richard Casserley, Ray East, the late Geoff Gamble, John Gerchen, the late David Jackson, John Parnham, Ron Potter, the late Stephen Gradidge, Tony Newman, Les Reason, Colin Seabright, Ron White/Colour-Rail, www.Tubeprune, Dewi Williams and any to whom I have been unable to give due credit. I am also grateful to Orbit Press for copying and digitally restoring some of the poorer original images.

In parallel, the major collections have been fine sources of material and in particular, I greatly appreciate the support from Simon Murphy of London's Transport Museum Photo Archive (LTM), Carl Anderson – Curator of Leicestershire, Leicester & Rutland Record Office (LLRRO) – in relation to the Newton Archive, the LCGB/Ken Nunn Collection, the National Railway Museum Photo Archive, the Brent Archive, the J L Smith-'Len's of Sutton Collection' (LOSC), the Sheffield Local Studies Library, Watford Central Library, and images from Metronet, Bombardier and Chiltern Railways.

As before, the Met & GC Joint Committee records at the London Metropolitan Archive have proved to be an invaluable source of primary material and thanks must also go to the Centre for Buckinghamshire Studies (CfBS) under Roger Bettridge as well as the local libraries at Chesham, Chorleywood, Wendover and Rickmansworth. Geoff Saul of the Rickmansworth Local History Society kindly drew my attention to the early *Financial News* report. However, pure records must be interpreted in the light of experience and here I remain indebted to 'Joint' railwaymen such as Richard Hardy, Tony Geary, Don Grant and a host of others who have tried to set me on the right path. As before, I am indebted to that fine railway artist Peter Green who created the atmospheric cover painting and Archie Eager, whose printers produced a result better than I deserved. Finally, the kind assistance of Elizabeth Foxell, Len Bunning and Peter Cowan in checking the proofs is much appreciated, but any slips remain my responsibility.

CAF

CONTENTS

Throughout this book, the Metropolitan Railway is referred to as the 'Met' and all the phases of London Transport, from LPTB to LUL, generically as 'LT'.

CHAPTER 1

OVERTURE AND BEGINNERS

The Metropolitan Railway coined the word Metro-land at the beginning of the 20th century, to promote the relatively rural land to the north-west of London for housing convenient for their trains, thus increasing passengers. All of the elements of a desirable countryside, low-cost housing and easy access to work in London were essential to the success of the venture. The first part of this book deals with the surprisingly ad hoc manner in which the small London underground Metropolitan Railway came to be in such a favourable position. The second part of this book covers the origins and evolution of Metro-land itself.

The strange set of circumstances that culminated in the evolution of the Metropolitan Railway (Met) have been well documented elsewhere and therefore only a few illustrative aspects are touched upon here. However, I believe that my earlier books were probably the first to bring out the strong influence of the Met & GC Joint Committee. Through this the Great Central Railway (GCR) shared with the Met the detailed control of the railways through Metro-land.

If one person was responsible for the expansion of the Met from its humble origins in London, it was Sir Edward Watkin, who exerted an enigmatic influence over the railway industry during the second half of the Victorian era, and also cast a shadow over his shareholders. Much has been written recently about him which gives proper emphasis to his sweeping range of interests in politics, international trade and transport, but it seems unlikely now that we will ever understand properly the reasons behind many of his apparently quixotic actions. The few records that we have of his conversations and personal correspondence reveal a hyperactive, arrogant, dictatorial, acerbic, self-made and status-conscious person. In contrast with his predecessors such as the Stephensons and Brunel, as a second-generation railway leader he was not an engineer. As with other subjects, he usually had an intuitive opinion about innovations, but on specific technical matters, from signalling and choice of locomotives, or AC versus DC electrification, his decisions could often be misguided.

Watkin's main interests were influenced by the experiences of the earlier part of his life. Born in 1819, he became involved unwillingly in his father's business as a modest Manchester merchant, which showed him the opportunities of trade, but determined him to be in charge of any future ventures. However, the other main

The makers of Metro-land. Top right: Sir Edward Watkin, who drove the Met Extension to the north west of London. Top left: Robert Selbie, who used Watkin's inheritance to create Metro-land. Mid right: Charles Liddell the engineer and left, Joseph Firbank the contractor who built the railway. Bottom right: Frank Pick the Managing Director and left, Lord Ashfield, the Chairman of London Transport, who inherited Metro-land. *(LTM)*

preoccupation of his father, namely politics, strongly caught his imagination and he became very active in local affairs. The other trait that he took from his father (who rather looked down on his wife) was sensitivity over status. Later, when hoping to marry, he realised that he needed the income from a steady job and became Secretary to the Trent Valley Railway (TVR) which was to lead to him to the top of this blossoming industry. In retrospect, perhaps his father, who took him as a boy to see the opening of the Liverpool & Manchester Railway in 1830, also influenced this. Fortunately for Watkin, the TVR turned out to be a desirable strategic acquisition for the powerful London & North Western Railway (LNWR) and, by facilitating the take-over, he rose to become a senior administrator with the parent company. However, his obsession with work, which was to be a feature of the rest of his life, now became apparent, and a near breakdown resulted in an extended 'rest' in the USA. The impact of the American meritocracy and 'can-do' culture, plus the scale of their activities, left a lasting impression on Watkin. On his return to the LNWR he became a key negotiator with the other major railways, revealing an ability to charm – when he wanted to – against his nature. In 1854 he became General Manager of the Manchester, Sheffield & Lincolnshire Railway (MS&LR), before being sent by the Government to Canada to advise on the future of the Hudson Bay Company and the Dominion. This led to his Chairmanship of the Grand Trunk Railway across Canada, which again encouraged the scale of his vision for railways and trade, and renewing his political interests. On returning to Britain and the MS&LR, Watkin became Chairman in 1864 (remaining so for some 30 years). On the strength of his performance, he joined the boards of numerous other railway companies and became involved in many ventures here and abroad. Of particular relevance to this story are his control, in effect, of the destinies of the MS&LR, Met, Aylesbury & Buckingham Railway (A&BR), East London Railway (ELR), South Eastern Railway (SER), Submarine Continental Railway Company, Chemin de Fer du Nord and the Wembley Tower Company.

The political ramifications of the often controversial activities of these companies fuelled Watkin's existing interest in politics. He was an MP from 1863 for periods over the next 25 years, during which he was characteristically autocratic and combative in lobbying and debate. This is illustrated in the description of the building of Marylebone Station in Chapter 5. Knighted in 1868, he associated with those who influenced matters, forming a friendship with Gladstone, with whom he shared religious interests, in order to sway decisions in his favour. But Watkin's egotistical and bellicose behaviour created many enemies who blocked his railway ambitions: in particular, his alienation of James Staats Forbes of the Metropolitan District Railway that delayed the creation of the Inner Circle. They were also in confrontation over the competition between Watkin's SER and Forbes's London Chatham & Dover Railway, thereby frustrating an obvious merger – to the disadvantage of almost everyone. Surprisingly, Watkin created considerable loyalty amongst his employees, perhaps because they felt he was defending their company like a feudal baron protecting those inside his castle, but he told them little of his plans.

This secretiveness had always been a feature of Watkin's business behaviour, for in any situation he liked to have a variety of options open to him, rather like playing cards, so that he could select a preferred strategy but change it according to prevailing conditions. And if others were unaware of his intentions, then they could not object to them! The later part of his career was dominated by the application of this approach to his culminating goal of creating a railway from Manchester to Paris to further international trade. Building on the patchwork of railways he controlled, he almost succeeded, however even in failure, he anticipated later developments and made Metro-land possible.

The heart of Watkin's empire was the Manchester, Sheffield & Lincolnshire Railway, which had originated in 1835 with the building of the notoriously difficult Woodhead tunnel through the Pennines, to link Manchester and Sheffield. To attract east-west trade, the railway was extended by means of amalgamation and construction to Lincoln, to access the east coast at Grimsby. But the main business came from the nearby central coal fields, transporting their output over other railways to the south of England, to satisfy the growing demand. In this expansion, the hub of Watkin's network came, somewhat surprisingly, to be the short underground Metropolitan Railway in central London. Born out of a concern by Charles Pearson, the City Solicitor, about the extreme congestion in the streets from horse-drawn traffic, cattle being driven to slaughter, barrows, and pedestrians, he proposed in 1830 a 'railway arcade' under London to alleviate matters. This was at a time when many thought that an underground railway would 'thereby disturb the devil'. Thirty years of persistent lobbying and attempting to raise the finance eventually led to the building of the Met beneath the New Road, linking the main line railway termini from Paddington to Farringdon in 1863. What now follows describes the construction and opening of this railway, because this was later to be the launching platform for Watkin's dreams and yet, in many ways, turned out to be a limiting factor in their realisation.

ooooo0000ooooo

CHAPTER 2

FOUNDATIONS OF THE MET IN LONDON
- the first underground steam railway

Charles Dickens in *Dombey and Son* gives the following contemporary description that sets the scene: -

"The first shock of a great earthquake had, just at that period, rent the whole neighbourhood to its centre. Traces of its course were visible on every side. Houses were knocked down; streets broken through and stopped; deep pits and trenches dug in the ground; enormous heaps of earth and clay thrown up; buildings that were undermined and shaking, propped by great beams of wood. Here, a chaos of carts, over-thrown and jumbled together, lay topsy-turvey at the bottom of a steep unnatural hill; there, confused treasures of iron soaked and rusted in something that had accidentally become a pond. Everywhere were bridges that led nowhere; thoroughfares that were wholly impassable; Babel towers of chimneys, wanting half their height; temporary wooden houses and enclosures, in the most unlikely situations; carcasses of ragged tenements, and fragments of unfinished walls and arches, and piles of scaffolding and wildernesses of bricks, and giant forms of cranes, and tripods straddling above nothing. There were a hundred thousand shapes and substances of incompleteness, wildly mingled out of their places, upside down, burrowing in the earth, aspiring in the air, mouldering in the water, and unintelligible as any dream. Hot springs and fiery eruptions, the usual attendants upon earthquakes, lent their contributions of confusion to the scene. Boiling water hissed and heaved within dilapidated walls, whence also, mounds of ashes blocked up rights of way, and wholly changed the law and custom of the neighbourhood.

In short, the yet unfinished and unopened railway was in progress; and from the very core of all this disorder, tailed smoothly away upon its mighty course of civilisation and improvement.

But, as yet, the neighbourhood was shy to own the railway. One or two bold speculators had projected streets; and one had built a little, but had stopped among the mud and ashes to consider further of it. A brand-new tavern, redolent of fresh mortar and size, and fronting nothing at all, had taken for its sign The Railway Arms; but that might be a rash enterprise — and then it hoped to sell drink to

The Metropolitan Railway was the first underground steam railway and it was mainly built just below the surface of the New Road to join a number of the London main line stations. Largely constructed by manual labour, a trench was dug for the tracks, covered by a brick arch and then the road surface relaid. *(Clive Foxell/ Orbit Press)*

Although the 'cut and cover ' method was an easier technique than deep level tunnelling, it could cause serious problems in built-up areas, as above with the extensive subsidence at Coppice Row in Clerkenwell. The worst incident was when the underground River Fleet, a virtual sewer, was breached by the excavations.

On 30th August 1862, construction was sufficiently advanced for an inspection train to run on the Met. It was arranged by the contractors, Smith & Knight, using their wagons and some GWR broad-gauge coaches, and is here seen about to enter Portland Road station. The waving is either excitement or relief from emerging from the fumes. *(ILN)*

workmen. So, the Excavators' house of Call had sprung up from a beer- shop: and the old-established ham and beef shop had become the Railway Eating House, with roast leg of pork daily, through interested motives of a similar immediate and popular description. Lodging-house keepers were favourable in like manner, and for the like reasons not to be trusted. The general belief was very slow. There were frowzy fields, and cow-houses, and dunghills, and dust heaps, and ditches and gardens, and summerhouses, and carpet-beating grounds, at the very door of the railway. A little tumuli of oyster shells in the oyster season, and lobster shells in the lobster season, and broken crockery and faded cabbage leaves in all seasons, encroached upon its high places. Posts, and rails and old cautions to trespassers, and backs of mean houses, and patches of wrecked vegetation, stared it out of countenance. Nothing was better for it, or thought of being so. If miserable waste ground lying near it could have laughed, it would have laughed it to scorn, like many of its miserable neighbours."

The engineer responsible for the construction of the Met was the eminent Sir John Fowler, but in practice he delegated most of the difficult tunnelling work to Benjamin Baker, who employed the 'cut and cover' method, excavating a large trench for the tracks and then bricking an arch over it. Although most of the route was laid just beneath the Marylebone, Euston and Farringdon Roads to minimise disruption, there were places as described above, particularly near the Fleet River (or rather sewer), that involved much demolition work.

What follows is based on a contemporary description of the first day of operation of the Met, from *The Times* newspaper of 11th January 1863.

"Yesterday the underground Metropolitan Railway was opened to the public, and many thousands were enabled to indulge their curiosity in reference to this mode of travelling under the streets of the metropolis. The trains commenced running as early as six o'clock in the morning from Paddington station, and the Farringdon–street terminus, in order to accommodate workmen, and there was a goodly muster of that class of the public, who availed themselves of the advantages of the line in reaching their respective places of employment. At eight o'clock the desire to travel underground in the direction of the City began to manifest itself at various stations along the line, and by nine it became equally evident to the authorities that neither the locomotive power nor rolling stock at their disposal was at all in proportion to their requirements of the opening day. From this time, and throughout the morning every station became crowded with anxious travellers who were admitted in sections; but poor were the chances of those who ventured to take their tickets before Baker-street, as the occupants were mainly 'long distance', or passengers for the terminus. This tended to increase the numbers at every station by the minute and we believe

that ultimately a number of Great Western Railway narrow gauge carriages as well as engines were brought in to accommodate the public.

Possibly the greatest point of attraction was King's Cross, which is certainly the finest station on the line, throwing even the termini into the shade. At this point in the morning, the crowds were immense, and as trains arrived a cry of "No Room" went up, having a depressing effect on the crowds. Between eleven and twelve, at this station, the money takers refused to take money for journeys between King's Cross and Farringdon, but issued tickets only to Paddington. However, many whose destination was the City, and were determined to ride on the opening day, took tickets for the opposite direction, in order to secure places for the return journey. At twelve o'clock the clerks informed the 500 or 600 who were then assembled at King's Cross, that there were enough people at Paddington to fill four trains in succession and therefore their instructions were to issue no Farringdon tickets for an hour. This had the effect of getting rid of very large numbers.

Thus during the morning the tendency was for traffic towards Farringdon and the public could proceed westwards with little inconvenience, but in the afternoon the tide set in the other way and the approaches to the trains at Victoria-street can be compared to the crush at the doors for the first night of a pantomime. Between one and two o'clock, thousands of anxious travellers for the new route were collected outside the Victoria-street terminus, and when the outer doors were opened, the rush was tremendous, and on reaching the ticket office the difficulty of exchanging cash for ticket was equally difficult. The platform gained the next grand struggle was for a seat in the outgoing train. Classification was altogether ignored, the holders of first's being compelled to go in third's or not at all, and vice versa. Hundreds on each occasion had to be left behind, to take their chance on the next train. Once in motion, all appeared to be right, the riding was very easy, and a train which left Farringdon-street at 2.15 reached King's-cross station at 2.18 (a little over a mile). Gower-street was reached at 2.25, Portland-road at 2.30, Baker-street at 2.36, Edgware-road at 2.42, and the terminus at Paddington at 2.48; thus performing the journey in 33 mins, including stoppages at the various stations. Other journeys took over 40 mins, but this was due to the excitement of the public to get places, and the running about of officials at every station to each carriage to see if there was a seat for one here and two there, no doubt took up more than half the time which would be occupied by the stoppage of a train at each station on ordinary occasions.

Of the general comfort in travelling there can be no doubt, and the novel introduction of gaslight into the carriages is calculated to dispel any unpleasant feelings which passengers, especially ladies, might entertain against riding for so long a distance through a tunnel. Yesterday, throughout every journey, the gas burnt brightly, and in some instances was turned so strong in the first-class carriages, in each of which there were two burners, that when the carriages were stationary, newspapers could be read with facility; but, in motion, the draught created so much flickering as to render it difficult. The second-class carriages are very nicely fitted with leather seats, and are very commodious, and the compartments and arms in the first-class render overcrowding impossible.

There is one point to which attention was adversely attracted, and that was that it was understood that there was to be no steam or smoke from the engines used in working this tunnel railway. All we can say is, that on one of the journeys between Portland-road and Baker-street, not only were the passengers enveloped in steam, but they were subjected to the unpleasantness of smoke also. This may have arisen because the pressure on the workers of the Metropolitan line who were compelled to avail themselves of locomotives as well as rolling stock of the Great Western Railway, and this is only a temporary inconvenience. Up to six o'clock it is estimated that about 25,000 persons had been carried over the line, and it is gratifying that, notwithstanding the eagerness of the public to get in the carriages, even when the trains were in motion, no single accident, of any kind, was reported."

The report refers to the use of GWR locomotives hauling the first trains. This arose because the GWR had eventually subscribed a significant sum to enable the Met to be built, probably because they wished to improve access from the City to their, then distant, Paddington. A condition of this support was that the Met should be laid with both standard and broad gauge tracks to enable GWR trains to use the underground lines. As it happened this was fortuitous, as Fowler's novel smokeless locomotive for the Met was a failure and Gooch of the GWR was able to provide some condensing tank engines at the last moment. However, in the first of many further occasions a disagreement broke out between the two companies and the Met had to quickly buy some existing standard designs, with added condensing gear from Beyer-Peacock. These so-called A & B class tank engines remained the mainstay of the Met for many years, but smoke emission remained such a serious problem that local chemists sold a patent elixir called the 'Metropolitan Mixture' to alleviate the effects of the sulphurous atmosphere.

In fact some 40,000 passengers were successfully carried on this first day and 225,000 in the week, and this growth continued without serious incident, with the traffic reaching some 15 million a year in 1865. In the light of these encouraging results, the Met was extended west to Hammersmith in 1864, south to South Kensington by 1868 and, significantly to the north, by association with a physically unconnected primitive single-track branch from Baker Street in a tunnel to Swiss Cottage.

oooooOOOOOooooo

CHAPTER 3

WATKIN TAKES OVER AND PUSHES NORTH (AND SOUTH)

At this time, Watkin had been involved in numerous railway projects abroad and in Britain, but the affairs of his MS&LR and SER predominated. To say that they were the most important in his mind at all times would be wrong, for he was able to compartmentalise his time and energies and do the equivalent of 'keeping all his irons in the fire at the same time'. However, there was always one theme in his mind against which he examined all emerging railway developments – and that was his passion for a rail link between his home town of Manchester and Paris, which he regarded as the doorway to European trade. Indeed, Hamilton Ellis described it 'as part of a North Country plot to capture Continental Europe'! Watkin was notoriously secretive about such intentions, probably reflecting his desire to acquire enterprises without fuss and at low cost, so that he could at the right juncture assemble the pieces to form a design that only he knew. In this turmoil of parallel negotiations, he fraternised with any relevant competitor, land owner, financier or politician and continually changed tack to achieve his ends.

Another piece of his jigsaw was to fall into place when the Met ordinary shareholders, who were in the majority, became increasingly uneasy about the financial performance of their investment. This arose from the substantial legal costs over disputes with the GWR and the then Metropolitan District Railway (MDR), who had built a line parallel to the Met nearer the Thames, and were competing with them over joining up to produce an 'Inner Circle'. Secondly, they noticed from the accounts that various expenses and contractors' charges were being treated as capital and this was also being used to subsidise the high dividend payments. Following further revelations of malpractice, the larger shareholders became apprehensive and a group from Manchester, led by Henry Pochin, inserted fellow Mancunian Edward Watkin as Chairman in 1872. He immediately shed several of the 'old guard' and brought in replacements from the north, including John Bell of his MS&LR as Secretary. His stringent review of accounting practices and expenses led to abrasive meetings with the company's contractors, lawyers and consultants, but resulted in a recovery of the share price and a more realistic dividend policy.

Watkin's railway empire was centred on the Manchester, Sheffield & Lincolnshire Railway – widely known as 'the Sheffield'. In 1875, Sheffield Victoria station is en fête with the arrival of the pilot engine (Sacré 2-4-0 class 24 no.153) before the Royal Train with the Prince and Princess of Wales. *(Head of Leisure, Sheffield Local Studies Library)*

Watkin also acquired the Wotton Tramway in deepest Bucks as part of his empire. This was built in 1872 by the 3rd Duke of Buckingham to serve his estate and he is seen here (to the right), beside his Aveling & Porter geared locomotive – of traction engine origins – which replaced the horses that first worked the primitive railway. *(LLRRO)*

The Wotton Tramway meandered from Quainton Road, on the A&BR (another of the Duke of Buckingham's interests), almost to the town of Brill, via a 'station' shown here at Wotton. Like most of the stations on this line, it was very basic with a short single platform and simple siding. *(LLRRO)*

Also near Wotton was this quaint water tower for replenishing the engines. The ladder was to enable the lad to refill it with a bucket from the adjacent stream. As can be seen, the financial state of the railway meant that the track was always in poor condition, resulting in frequent derailments. *(LLRRO)*

Westcott was another station on the Brill branch, built by the Duke to serve his own gasworks. By the time Watkin controlled the line, the crude Aveling & Porter engines had been replaced by two small second-hand Manning Wardle tank locomotives. Here one hauls a mixed train of a retired Met Oldbury 8-wheeled coach and wagons. *(LLRRO)*

The Duke had ambitions to upgrade his private line as part of a railway extending to Oxford. Inevitably this attracted Watkin, who saw possibilities for the Met and acquired this proposed Oxford & Aylesbury Tramway. The track was improved, but not extended, and at Quainton Road only this coach remained as evidence of the idea. *(LLRRO)*

The opening of the Extension stretched the A class engines intended for the Inner Circle and Watkin arranged for the designs by Stirling for his SER to be given to Neilson & Co to supply the C class 0-4-4T's. At Finchley Road in the 1890s, no.69 pauses on the way to Aylesbury, whilst the guard has left his 4-wheeled brake van. *(Stephen Gradidge Col.)*

Also in the 1890s, at Neasden & Kingsbury station in the open countryside and with milk churns on the platform, an Aylesbury-bound train on the right approaches, headed by a stalwart 4-4-0T A class Met engine. It is passing a C class no.67 for Baker Street with a rake of rough riding, Oldbury rigid 8-wheeler coaches. *(Stephen Gradidge Coll.)*

For Watkin, control of the Met fitted in perfectly with his earlier appointment as the Receiver (and then Chairman in 1868) of the East London Railway (ELR), which later gave him a link from the Met, through Brunel's Thames Tunnel, to his SER at New Cross. However, these moves also escalated his bitter personal conflicts with James Staats Forbes, who was the equally confrontational Chairman of both the London Chatham & Dover Railway, competing for south coast traffic, and the Metropolitan District Railway, battling over the Inner Circle. In retrospect, this war of attrition between them did little for their passengers or shareholders and often diverted Watkin's energies from his main objective of creating a railway between Manchester and Paris. Nevertheless, in 1870 he was able to take control of the various existing proposals for building a rail tunnel under the English Channel by becoming Chairman of the Submarine Continental Railway Company. Therefore, as a result of these multifarious acquisitions, by the mid 1870s he could comfort himself that he had in place the crucial elements of such a railway. In the north he had the MS&LR, in London the Met, now connected by the ELR under the River Thames to his SER at New Cross. From the SER at Folkestone, his Channel Tunnel was to be dug to Calais and thence, by his Chemin de Fer du Nord, to his objective of Paris!

However, the glaring hole in this scheme lay between the MS&LR in Nottingham and the Met at Baker Street. But being Watkin, he had for years been cultivating many options for closing this gap. As usual, he preferred to start with the cheapest alternative of acquiring a bankrupt railway, then sharing another railway line or just obtaining running powers over it, before the last resort of building one of his own. In this case, from the London end in the south, the first step was to acquire the related Baker St. - St John's Wood - Swiss Cottage line (1883) and extend it via a shadow company to Harrow and Rickmansworth (1887), whence in parallel he explored: (1) a joint company with the LNWR to Tring to get access to their mainline to the north; (2) a new railway through High Wycombe; and (3) a new line to Chesham. The latter could still join the LNWR or be extended to Aylesbury. As always, he 'wheeled and dealed' with the relevant influential politicians, financiers and landowners such as Gladstone and Disraeli, the Rothschilds, and the Dukes of Buckingham and Bedford – who were all often involved in railway negotiations. Eventually following option (3), Watkin reached Aylesbury in 1892. Then by acquiring another impoverished company, the Aylesbury & Buckingham Railway, from the Duke of Buckingham and Sir Harry Verney, the Met was only some 93 miles from the MS&LR in the north. Equally, in a typically lateral move, Watkin took a major interest in the adjoining private estate railway of the Duke of Buckingham, becoming a director in 1875, supporting its pretension to be the Oxford & Aylesbury Tramway for his own ends. This ramshackle light railway from Quainton Road to Brill had brave plans to reach Oxford, but in spite of the much later intervention of Col. H F Stephens – that saviour of hopeless railways – it remained just a rural byway.

From the north, in 1883, Watkin obtained the agreement in principle to the MS&LR completing the link with the Met and running their trains into Baker Street, and began scheming with his engineer, Liddell, over possible routes. There followed much bargaining with possible allies along the intended line who could generate more east-west traffic to bolster that from the mainly rural route, but eventually these negotiations collapsed and construction began on the direct connection with the Met at Quainton Road.

At the London end, Watkin was forced to admit that Baker Street station could not cope with the volume of trains of both companies and planned a grand new terminus for the MS&LR at Marylebone. This was to have an underground link to the eastbound Met line so that trains from Manchester could still traverse London and enter his SER, bound for Folkestone, then France and so to Paris!

ooooo0000ooooo

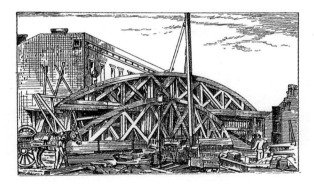

Contemporary drawing of Firbank building the skew bridge, at Brondesbury, for the Met.
(McDermott)

CHAPTER 4

CONSTRUCTING THE 'EXTENSIONS'

The main builders of the Met Extension, which was later to form the foundations of Metro-land, were Charles Liddell, a leading consulting engineer, and Joseph Firbank, a dependable and successful contractor. Brought together by mutual experiences in the explosive growth of the railway system in Britain, they came from completely different backgrounds. Together they participated in the radical changes that occurred in railway development during the 19th century, starting from the volatility, violence and manual construction methods associated with the early speculators, to the later emergence of the larger contractors using the new mechanical aids to build the railways.

Charles Liddell was born in 1812 into the ecclesiastical wing of the family and thus was to be an uncle to Alice Liddell, the inspiration for Alice in Lewis Carroll's *Alice in Wonderland*. However, after an education at Shrewsbury, his career took a different path when he became a pupil of the famous railway pioneer, George Stephenson, in 1830. There is little doubt that this came about through the influence of a scion of the family, Sir Thomas Liddell (later Earl of Ravensworth), who with Sir Stuart Wortley and the Earl of Strathmore, were known as 'the Grand Alliance' for their domination of the coal industry of Tyneside. Sir Thomas had been vital to George Stephenson's career, by being the first to order a working steam locomotive ('Blucher') from him for the Killingworth Colliery in 1814. Later, when George's wife died, he asked a niece (Eleanor) to be his housekeeper and she then married a Stephen Liddell, who worked in the Stephenson factory. When Stephen was subsequently killed by an accident at the works, Stephenson started to support the family and as a result Charles Liddell was taken into his firm.

However, it was George Stephenson's more accomplished son, Robert, who gave Charles Liddell his first real opportunity as a railway civil engineer. He employed him on the building of the Syston & Peterborough Railway, during which their 'prize fighters' battled with the stalwarts of the local landowner, Lord Harborough, at the notorious 'Battle of Saxby' in 1845, so that Liddell could complete his survey. This job was to be crucial because not only did it introduce him to the burgeoning and volatile world of railway construction, but it led to the building of the Leicester & Swannington Railway for the LNWR in 1846, where he met and impressed a rising LNWR manager, one Edward Watkin. Later, in 1853, Liddell created a consulting engineering practice with I D B Gordon, based at Westminster, to be on hand for the parliamentary activities that formed a significant aspect of their work. Together they constructed some 14 railways in Britain, including in 1852-4 the Newport, Abergavenny & Hereford line and also the Taff Vale Railway, which included the spectacular Crumlin viaduct. Liddell also established a substantial overseas practice, being responsible for the Danube & Black Sea line in Turkey (another of Watkin's foreign ventures), as well as the Novara & Lake Orta Railway in Italy.

In common with other consulting engineers of that time, Liddell was involved in a wide range of disciplines. For example, he became a partner in R Newall & Co., wire cable manufacturers, and was involved in laying the telegraph cable from Varna to Balaclava across the Black Sea during the Crimean War of 1854-6, and then cables in the Mediterranean, totalling some 4,000 miles in length.

Such widespread activities again led Liddell to the notice of Edward Watkin, who had agitated for more professional engineers to be used to improve the efficiency of pursuing the chaotic Crimean War, but had declined a request from Lord Palmerston to take charge personally of the reorganisation. Later Watkin became interested in reviving the failing Grand Trunk Railway in Canada and, on becoming chairman, asked Liddell to produce plans for bridging the St Lawrence at Montreal. Then Watkin became publicly increasingly disenchanted with the alleged extravagance of Sir John Fowler as consulting engineer to both the Met and the MS&LR. As a consequence, Liddell replaced Fowler in 1873 at the same retainer of £100 p.a. and immediately became immersed in MS&LR projects such as the building of the Derbyshire and Nottinghamshire lines. Watkin began to use him on more speculative ventures, like suggesting how to ease the congestion at Grimsby Docks, although Liddell's proposal for a new dock at Immingham was not taken up until Sam Fay later came to power. As chairman of the SER, Watkin also involved Liddell in his plan to develop Dungeness as a major port to further his cross-channel ambitions, and also as a director of his Wembley Tower project to judge the design competition for the structure.

By now Liddell had a substantial practice with teams of surveyors, negotiators, inspectors and resident engineers in the field with both the Met and the MS&LR. The basis of these contracts is of interest: 'to be paid £350 per mile of line, to include stations of an ordinary nature. If required to design or superintend any large station works, locomotive shops, etc. – they will not be included'. They also excluded the services of his resident engineer, inspectors and clerk of works. Liddell's main tasks for Watkin increasingly centred on the implementation of his desired link between the MS&LR and the Met. In this role Liddell not only undertook the surveys, planned the route and construction, but also recommended the contractors and their payment; all through his own large team of engineers and inspectors. But probably of more significance, he advised Watkin on the options available for the purchase of the necessary land for the line, on likely competitors and the relevant parliamentary ramifications. In these respects, he was probably closer than any other associate to knowing the secretive Watkin's real intentions.

However, there were few options for the route of the first extension of the Met from Baker Street over the St John's Wood branch to the major town of Harrow because of the terrain, and Watkin had already negotiated the purchase of much of the land. Nevertheless, the earthworks were formidable and here Liddell was to rely as the contractor on the redoubtable Firbank, who had impressed him on earlier projects, and with whom he would now collaborate on most of the following work. From the late 1880s Watkin became increasingly preoccupied with the political and financial ramifications of his great vision and the choice of the route beyond Harrow to the north, and the MS&LR at Annesley. As a result, Liddell, being familiar with Watkin's objectives and entrepreneurial approach to achieving them, gradually took more initiative in seeking solutions and responsibility for pursuing negotiations with the principals of those involved. Equally, as Watkin's health declined, his iron control of the Met and MS&LR weakened so that Liddell had more direct access to their Boards.

At Rickmansworth, Liddell had tried unsuccessfully to obtain land from an obdurate John Birch, a director of the Bank of England, and was thus forced to divert the tracks in a sharp curve around his estate. Ironically, Birch and his family later became avid users of the Met but, even today, this bend hinders the speed of trains through the station and makes a difficult start to the climb up the Chilterns. Then taking a route for the railway to Chalfont Road, that gave Liddell the best option of later avoiding the objections of the Tyrwhitt-Drakes at Old Amersham and for going on to Aylesbury. But in the interim he planned to extend the line by first descending the Chess Valley to Chesham, then extending to Tring – if Watkin's manoeuvres with the LNWR succeeded. After Watkin 'persuaded' the townspeople of Chesham to pay to have a station convenient for their town, Liddell surveyed a route to Tring along the Vale and bought some parcels of land. However, the LNWR attitude changed and after Chesham was reached in 1889, Liddell pushed the main line west via the River Misbourne valley on to Aylesbury in 1892.

As early as mid-1882, Liddell had been exploring the routes beyond Aylesbury from both the Met and the MS&LR perspectives, and had presented a number of alternative schemes before both Boards, which reflected Watkin's ever-changing preoccupations. However, the obvious candidate for moving north from Aylesbury was the impoverished A&BR line to Quainton Road – which Watkin had been

An early picture of the exterior of Harrow-on-the-Hill station, opened in 1880 and designed with a hint of Queen Anne style to reflect the importance of the town. Equally, this main entrance was on Lowlands Road for convenience to the School. The smell from horse-drawn cabs in the large yard on the right caused many complaints! *(LOSA)*

The Station Master and staff of the Joint pose for a photo on Pinner station, beside the early type of Met station name board. As they passed, the engine crews would take the opportunity for a quick glance up Pinner High Street, in order to check their progress against the Church clock. In many ways the station looks much the same today. *(LOSA)*

Some 3 miles beyond Pinner, the service to Northwood started in 1887 and although few people lived in the vicinity, the Met Board noted that most of the 53 building plots adjacent to the station were sold within a few months. The later impact of Metro-land can be seen by comparing this scene with that at the bottom of page 132. *(LOSA)*

Further on at Rickmansworth, Liddell was unable to acquire the land he wished and had to divert the railway line in a regrettably sharp curve through the station, before a steep climb up the Chilterns. Here, a down Met train enters, with a rake of rigid 8-wheeler Oldbury coaches hauled by a class A 4-4-0 tank engine, no.45. *(Ray East Collection)*

A similar Met train to the previous picture approaches Chalfont Road (Junction for Chesham) in the 1890s. As with many early Met stations, the elaborate awnings seem the most important feature and were certainly needed in the exposed heights of the Chilterns. Note the amount of luggage, mail and parcels being dealt with.*(Ray East Coll.)*

From Chalfont the Extension was built to Chesham in 1889, in the hope of continuing on to the LNWR at Tring. But Watkin's scheming came to naught and the prosperous town of Chesham became the end of a single track branch. Here the line is being laid in a cutting through chalk, down to the Chess Valley at a gradient of 1 in 66. *(Ray East Coll.)*

The formal inspection of the line to Chesham on 18th May 1889, with VIPs posed in front of a Met first-class carriage of a train drawn by a Firbank engine. Banners reflecting the wait of over 50 years for the railway, proclaimed *'come at last!'*. A traditional banquet, with champagne, speeches and bands was held in the Goods Shed. *(Ray East Collection)*

Watkin's proposed route from Chesham to his LNWR friends at Tring was abandoned in favour of extending the line from Chalfont Road via Amersham, to Aylesbury. This is the scene at Ostler's Wood, north of Amersham, with tree clearance and the preparations for a large embankment, as described by the *Financial News* reporter on page 43. *(CfBS)*

Liddell had selected a route to avoid the Drake estates at Amersham and Firbank started working towards Aylesbury in 1891. This shows his 0-4-0T engine 'Caldew' at Mantles Green, just north of Amersham. In the foreground are piles of the steel sleepers that were used beyond Harrow. The navvies usually called them 'pig troughs'. *(Ray East Coll.)*

Following the completion of the link with the Great Central Railway in 1899, their trains began to use the Met Extension and stop at stations north of Harrow. Near the highest point of the Chilterns, such a train of just two coaches, hauled by a Robinson 4-4-2 class C13 tank engine, enters Great Missenden station bound for Marylebone. *(LOSA)*

With Firbank's upgrade of the A&BR, a new Aylesbury station was shared with a reluctant GWR. This 1897 picture shows the Met line joining from the left, and that of the GWR line from Risborough from the right. In 1906, the two owners were replaced by Joint companies with the GCR, and it thus became a complex tripartite station. *(LLRO)*

After Aylesbury, Liddell had arranged for Firbank to upgrade the single-track of the A&BR, to reach the GCR at Quainton. This early picture shows the A&BR running from Aylesbury on the right, past the Quainton Road platform, north to the GCR. In front, a train on the Duke of Buckingham's Wotton Tramway heads for Brill. *(Clive Foxell Coll.)*

Quainton Road station, as later rebuilt by Firbank. Looking north, beyond the level crossing in the far distance, was the junction where the London Extension of the MS&LR connected with the Met line to the remote Verney Junction. To the far left is the platform used by what had been the Wotton Tramway and now operated by the Met. *(LLRO)*

The level crossing seen in the previous picture was soon replaced by a bridge in order to reduce the disruption to what was now a main line. This illustration shows a railwayman tending a new starter signal at the end of the down platform. As it is now just in front of the bridge, the brickwork has been painted white in order to improve visibility. *(LLRO)*

Firbank encouraged the Navvy Mission, for even in the 1890s the navvies had a bad reputation and lived 'rough', or in very primitive huts, near their work. Here, a group in their best clothes and with an accompanying brass band from the Navvy Mission at nearby Calvert is on a Sunday School outing to Quainton. *(LLRRO)*

At Upper South Farm Junction, just beyond Quainton Road, a small boy posed on the new tracks being built by the MS&LR to the south to join the Met about half a mile ahead under the new bridge. The original Met line from Aylesbury to Verney Junction via Grandborough Road and Winslow Road lies on the left. *(LLRRO)*

The GCR now joined the Met at Quainton Road, but the Met itself diverged over the upgraded A&BR, to Watkin's dream of a major interchange with the LNWR at Verney Junction. Winslow Road was an intermediate station, and is shown here in the 1890s with an up class C engine, hauling farming equipment and an Oldbury coach. *(CfBS)*

Verney Junction, named after Sir Harry Verney who provided the necessary land. The LNWR line to Oxford lies ahead, but they had been reluctant to grant interchange facilities with the A&BR. This 1902 view shows that Watkin had been able to arrange for Liddell and Firbank to improve the island platform for use by the Met. *(L&GRP)*

courting assiduously for years – and so Liddell surveyed it for an upgrade to main line use. Equally, the initial path of a new MS&LR south from Annesley was now clear, as the board had accepted Liddell's plans in 1883. But, whilst he was working near what was to become Chalfont Road, he became aware of a independent speculative scheme for a railway, north from there to Moreton Pinkney on the East & West Junction Railway, which would save him building some 45 miles of track. Liddell convinced Watkin to back this proposal and then to lobby hard for the enabling bill, but it failed and Liddell returned to his previous plan to link the A&BR with a new line via Brackley to the MS&LR. By 1890, Liddell's plans for upgrading the A&BR were approved by the Met and the MS&LR accepted those for the new line from Quainton Road to Annesley. He was then asked to implement the southern section, and an Edward Parry the northern one. However, in 1893 Liddell found it was difficult to finalise terms with the MS&LR board and, after much haggling, they instead appointed the firm of Sir Douglas & Francis Fox to take over the southern section of the new railway. To some, it has seemed odd that Liddell should part from Watkin in this way, but it may have been a welcome excuse. For Liddell, who had defined the MS&LR line to London using the larger continental clearances required by Watkin, must have been well aware of their incompatibility with the Met. Because of this, and perhaps his age, he may have found it a reason to depart. Soon afterwards, in 1894, Liddell died whilst at work in his office, aged 82 years.

His compatriot, **Joseph Firbank,** was born in 1819 at Bishop Auckland in Durham and, as his family were all miners, he joined them working underground in the pits at the age of 7 years old. Over the next few years he became expert in excavating and shoring tunnels, but fortunately he was encouraged to attend night classes by none other than the Rector of Easington, the Rev Henry Liddell, who was the father of Charles Liddell – later destined to be a leading railway engineer and collaborator with Joseph Firbank! As a result of his experience and education, Firbank's position rose at the Haswell & Hetton Collieries until he left to become a small contractor with his own team of navvies. His first significant project was working on the excavation of the pioneering 3 mile long Woodhead Tunnel through the millstone grit of the Pennines for the MS&LR. His fortitude during this extremely difficult task, integrity in his business dealings, a paternalistic attitude to his workforce, and control of costs were to become hallmarks of his future activities. It was his habit to keep a close eye on the progress of his contracts and he slept little, to the extent that a waiter at his favourite hotel remarked that *"it would have been simpler if Mr Firbank had combined dinner and breakfast"*. He also had a common-sense approach to all matters and, for example, where often a good estimate was the difference between success or failure, he used the simple rules such as *"that on a dry summer day one of his navies could excavate 5 cubic yards of earth a day and this needed to be matched by a supply of some 2 lbs. of meat, 2 lbs. of bread with 5 quarts of ale"*. He spent so much time supervising the work in progress that his appearance was more that of a ruddy-faced farmer.

Charles Liddell later wrote of him: *"I first came in contact with Mr Firbank in 1846 on the Syston & Peterborough Railway. He was then a sub-contractor, but afterwards completed the work of one of the contractors who failed. The next work in which he was engaged under me as engineer was the completion of the contract of Messrs. Dyson, on a 13½ mile section of the Rugby & Stamford line. He obtained great credit for the manner in which this work was executed and so I sometime afterwards introduced him to the Monmouth Railway Board (1854), and this was the commencement to his successful career as a contractor. He carried out all the alterations and deviations, and built the locomotive shops of that company, to the great satisfaction of the Board, and the ultimate benefit of the undertaking. He was afterwards engaged for many of the works on which I was engineer, and I always found him upright and conscientious in all dealings, and indomitable in overcoming difficulties and obstacles."*

Indeed, Liddell and Firbank mutually supported each other during their ongoing association. Initially, Liddell helped Firbank when he briefly entered into business with an untrustworthy partner, and later in the periods of financial difficulty due to the periodic collapse of banks or the stock market. Equally, Firbank always tried to do a professional job within his estimate and, if it cost more for good reason, Liddell was content to let Firbank argue his case and then accept the Director's decision. As he became more successful, Firbank was even prepared to invest his own money in railway schemes that were crucial to Liddell. Although Firbank had a long association with Liddell, much of his construction work was for other railways, notably on the Settle & Carlisle, the London Extension of the Midland Railway, lines in South Wales, as well as the Brighton and South Western companies.

When Watkin started to extend the Met from Swiss Cottage to Finchley Road in 1878, the contract was awarded to Firbank, thus renewing his association with their engineer Liddell. Firbank's son, Joseph Thomas, had joined the business in 1864 and was now taking a key role. The existing tunnel was extended by 'cut and cover' with the resulting spoil used for the embankment beyond Finchley Road. However, here the works were delayed by long spells of frost and rain, together with a shortage of burnt clay for ballasting the track, until Watkin ordered trainloads of shingle to be brought from the beach at his SER Dungeness port project. This caused Firbank much trouble and expense, resulting in his having to use 24-hour working in order to open the line to Willesden Green in 1879 for the Royal Agricultural Show. Appropriately, this station was still in the open countryside. From here, the line had an almost clear run to Harrow, but before Kilburn two fine bridges had to be built over major roads. The first, a 104 ft brick skew bridge at Brondesbury, was the largest brick span in Britain at the time. Again near Kilburn, two more skew bridges were erected, principally of cast-iron with wrought-iron cross girders. On the short section from Willesden to Harrow, Firbank built a two-arch bridge over the badly flooded River Brent by using dams. Last, but by no means least, was his iron bridge of 122 ft span crossing the LNWR's four-track main line to the north at Kenton. After crossing mainly open fields, Firbank was – in the light of his earlier doubtful reception by other scholastic towns – somewhat surprised to be welcomed to Harrow in 1880. For this section he was paid £272,000, which only just covered his costs.

Parliament had authorised the continuation of the Met Extension on to Rickmansworth in 1879, but surprisingly the contract was given to a William Maxwell. However, he badly underestimated the costs involved in the relatively flat terrain, due to the combination of unstable ground and heavy rain, particularly near Lord Ebury's Moor Park estate. This led to the Met and Firbank completing the task, laying track on steel sleepers, with Rickmansworth station opening in 1887. Sadly, Firbank had died after a short illness in 1886 aged 67 years, but his son Joseph Thomas, who had by now taken on most of the day-to-day responsibility, took over the company with the aid of his nephew, Ralph Firbank, and established their headquarters at London Bridge.

The onward route chosen by Watkin and Liddell now lay through Chalfont Road, nominally to Chesham, but with the option of Tring or Aylesbury as the final destination. Firbank's were given the contract, and whilst few major bridges were involved, the poor weather conditions again made the work very difficult. So Firbank dug several gravel pits on Chesham Moor to provide drainage material for the line. Equally, climbing the Chiltern Hills and descending the valley of the River Chess to Chesham itself necessitated balancing major cuttings through the chalk with massive embankments. As Watkin's hopes for a link with the LNWR at Tring faded, the Chesham line was built only as a single-track branch. Then Firbank's were given authorisation to build the line from Chalfont Road through Amersham and the Wendover Gap, over the scarp of the Chilterns and, down to Aylesbury. Here, Watkin's previous acrimony with the GWR resulted in the Met being excluded from their station at Aylesbury and forced Firbank's to build a temporary platform for the opening in 1892.

Earlier, Joseph Firbank had become a director of Watkin's Tower Company and later in 1896, his company won the contract to build the massive foundations for Watkin's Tower at Wembley and the related extensions at Wembley Park station to cope with the optimistic expectations for visitors. Work started in 1892.

Under Watkin, the Met had acquired the A&BR in 1891, as well as the related Oxford & Aylesbury Tramway. In 1895 it asked Firbank's to implement Liddell's original plans for upgrading the frail single-track line from Aylesbury to Quainton Road and Verney Junction to the new Met main line standards, as part of the push to join with the MS&LR. Liddell had died suddenly at his office in August 1894 and his junior partner, Edward Richards, supervised the contract which involved complete replacement with double track, proper stations (including a new one, Waddesdon Manor) and removal of 22 out of the 24 level crossings! The work for joining with the MS&LR was completed early in 1897, but the growing acrimony between the Met and the MS&LR during Watkin's illness prevented the latter's use of the junction until the end of 1898.

Earlier in 1894, Firbank's had also started on the last section of the MS&LR line into the new Marylebone station. Contract no.7 consisted of a 2 mile section from the Met at Canfield Place, mainly by 'cut and cover', but with some tunnelling near Lord's Cricket Ground and the Hampstead Baths. At one point it also involved a substantial girder bridge across the LNWR mainline. A lot of demolition and clearance was necessary near the terminus and here, Liddell's original plans were modified by Sir Douglas & Francis Fox, with a steel raft over the Regent's Canal, rather than a tunnel underneath. In practice, the work caused minimal disruption to the cricket at Lord's and successfully avoided breaching the Hampstead Baths some 6 ft above the tunnel, but created vast amounts of spoil that had to be removed over the Met for disposal at sites around London.

The link to the Met was quietly dropped and the grand opening of 'the last main line in Britain' at Marylebone station, which took place in 1899, marked the end of the long association of Liddell and Firbank with Watkin and his railways.

How the building of the Extension appeared to contemporaries is shown by the following extracts from a rather sceptical contribution by a reporter to the *Financial News* (a forerunner of the *Financial Times*) in 1886. Strangely, it makes no mention of the line to Chesham, which even then was a prosperous town of several thousand inhabitants:

"I received instructions from the editor to proceed to that forlorn region between Rickmansworth and Aylesbury to ascertain what was being done by way of connecting them by railway. My editor had handed me the shorthand report of the words of Sir Edward Watkin, recently uttered in his address to the shareholders of the Metropolitan Railway. He said, "Now, gentlemen, we are in this position today. We will take capital first and the capital account is practically closed, with the exception of a very small sum of money (£30,000) to make the whole of the Inner Circle complete. A very small sum of money will then complete the only part of the railway north of Harrow, which we intend to ask you to construct out of Metropolitan capital. At present, that railway is lying partly idle – because the work is not complete. But in a very few months that railway will be completed to Rickmansworth, and there we shall stop".

I went to Rickmansworth by the L&NWR and found that the Metropolitan Railway came to a sudden stop, standing 12 feet or so in the air, looking as if the terminus had been chopped off by a gigantic knife. It is certainly a fitting place to terminate a railway, being a specimen of a 'one horse town'. A leading businessman of the town said "whatever could have induced the Metropolitan to extend itself to Rickmansworth, has puzzled me more than I can contemplate it. The enthusiasts harp on about the opening of gravel pits and lime beds, but you will find that they are selling land to the Metropolitan for £254 an acre that normally would not fetch more than £18." But I asked if the railway was really going to be built and was told that it was already being marked out with pegs.

To observe this progress I drove one of the Financial News mail carts with my faithful lieutenant of the whip beside me along the Reading road. As far as the eye could reach there was nothing but broad acres, very broad, and woods. For an hour we rode, keeping the pegging for the new railway in sight, without seeing a soul until we came to Chorleywood which now has about eight houses. The pegging extends into Buckinghamshire, along the property of the Duke of Bedford. After entering Lord Chesham's property the railway pushes on to Amersham. Here, droves of ducks, that puzzled me immensely, waddled into little alleys, trying to clear the way for us to reach The Griffin. Houses are rented at 1/6d a week; men live to the age of 90 and never dream of going to London. Those who have ever visited the Metropolis are regarded with pride. A mile beyond Aylesbury, on the vast tract of property of Squire T. T. Drake, I found a Mr Gates, responsible to Mr Charles Liddell the Engineer, who commanded the pegging of the Met route from Aylesbury. These pegs are driven down about halfway about 20ft apart, every third one standing higher than the rest. Local people pull them out almost as fast as they are driven, but this still leaves a hole where it had been the day before. Through the woods the men mark the trees with strange hieroglyphics. Standing where we were, on an immense hill, we looked across an expanse of valley. "Where do you run from this height?" I asked. "Right across" he replied. "On a bridge?" I asked. "No, we'll fill it up with this hill" he replied.

The new railway, when it is built, will run through the property of the Butcher Brothers towards Missenden, then enter Lord Howe's estate and through that of Mrs Carrington and the McConnell's to Wendover, which belongs to Lord Rothschild. Finally it finds a much-needed resting-place in Aylesbury, where many are of the impression that the purchases of land for the new Metropolitan Railway were made on behalf of the Aylesbury & Buckingham Railway. And as I come to the end of my report, I must sum up all my investigations by pronouncing the project sheer madness."

ooooo0000ooooo

CHAPTER 5

ARRIVING AT THE TERMINUS

Based on extracts from *Our Railways* by John Pendleton, 1894.

"The traditions of fierce Parliamentary infighting in the early days of the railways were revived in the session of 1891, when Sir Edward Watkin, one of the busiest and versatile of men, not content with writing the Life of Alderman Cobden of Manchester, with discovering new coalfields, with buying Snowdon, with making arrangements for the erection of a Tower of Babel[1], and with pegging away at his Channel Tunnel project, strove, on behalf of the Sheffield Company, to get sanction for the construction of the new trunk line to London. The railway, it was proposed, should be practically an extension from the southern terminus of the MS&LR at Annesley, to Nottingham, Leicester, Rugby and Quainton Road, joining the Metropolitan Company's system, and getting direct access to the capital.

The line, estimated to cost £6 million, would, it was urged, not only give important advantages to industrial centres of Nottingham and Leicester, and open up much rural country, benefiting the agriculturist and the labourer, but would also provide a very necessary outlet for the traffic of the company from the great coalfield of South Yorkshire and East Derbyshire, and for the trade in fish and general merchandise that they had developed at Grimsby. Moreover, it was pointed out that the company, which had been obliged hitherto to "grin and bear it" while handing their traffic to other companies, would now "obtain the unrestricted use of 42½ miles of railway all round the metropolis and across the Thames into Kent and Sussex". It was a straightforward and apparently smooth and practical scheme. The line threatened to interfere with no vital interest. At Nottingham it promised to do the work of a vigorous sanitary reformer and demolish a mass of old property that would be better razed to the ground. In various parts of the route it offered substantial help in business to those engaged in coal, iron, lace, hosiery and leather.

Nor did it present any engineering difficulty, for with the exception of a tunnel, 3,000 yards long south of Rugby, the work of construction seemed to be easy. But

---

[1]This refers to Watkin's discovery of a coalfield in Kent whilst excavating the Channel Tunnel; making a path to the top of Snowdon to access his hotel and building a chalet nearby, where he entertained Gladstone and Lloyd George; and the construction of his Wembley Tower to rival that of Eiffel in Paris.

opposition soon roused itself from slumber. In the heart of the country protest was made by a baronet (who) emphatically declined to allow any railway within a mile of his mansion. The rival railway companies opposed the project; and the Great Northern Railway Company, holding that the MS&LR were breaking a fifty years' agreement between the two companies ....., showed persistent hostility to the scheme, fighting tooth and nail in Committee. Quite apart from the ordinary railway rivalry, strong opposition grew up. The intention was to make an ample terminus near Baker Street, between Euston and Paddington, to the west of Regent's Park. To get there it was calmly proposed that the line should cut through St John's Wood and skirt or dive beneath Lord's Cricket Ground. The residents of this part of London were indignant. All the lovers of cricket received a shock.

The Art colony held their meetings and signed a petition against the Bill. Thirty acres of precious land were to be converted into a railway depot. The line, ruthlessly making its way by valuable property, was to be "a line for the conveyance not only of passengers, but coal, manure, fish, and other abominations". Such vandalism was monstrous, and men of such fame as Mr Alma-Tadema, Mr J. McWhirter, and Mr Briton Riviere, with many others took part to protest against it.........

In the world of cricket Sir Edward Watkin's audacity filled every player with amazement – some with rage. It was suggested that the railway magnate should be interviewed by W. G. Grace, that he should be confronted by Spofforth, the demon bowler, and that if he did not prove amenable to their persuasiveness, then, as a last resource, Briggs, the Lancashire cricketer – who, according to an amusing article in the evening paper, had been promoted, "owing to the accuracy of his aim", from a professional bowler to an officer of artillery and Dictator of England – should cripple the ruthless baronet. The menace to Lord's was looked upon almost as a national calamity. Everybody who took an interest in cricket, who had been at Lord's in sunshine and shower, or who had read about the wonderful bowling, and batting, and fielding there, hated Sir Edward Watkin, and was prepared, at any hazard, to protect the sacred ground.

The thought of steel rails running through it was repellent. Ballast and sleepers, Bessemer tracks and signal-boxes, banging wagons and shrieks of engines seemed utterly alien to such a fine open space, hallowed by pleasant memories and by all that was best in cricket. The mind of many a player sped quite a century backward over the bridge of time, and recalled the early days of the Marylebone Club and the difficulty of obtaining the ground; how Thomas Lord, a sort of athletic jack-of-all-sport, bowled for the members of the club and secured a ground in Dorset Square and how, in 1814, the present site in St John's Wood was procured. So firm and fresh was the turf in Dorset Square that it was removed again to Lord's .... It was through this bulwark that the railway iconoclast intended to drive his engines. No such sacrilege had been contemplated since John Ruskin's wrath at the railway invasion of Derbyshire. There were people, indeed, who were inclined to apply the art critic's description of railway-making devastation to Sir Edward Watkin. They said he deserved to be seized by his own navvies and blown up by dynamite.

But, fortunately, no such fearful fate awaited him. Sir Edward Watkin, with the suavity which is one of his most conspicuous characteristics, soothed nearly all the indignant members of the club. He should be sorry indeed, he explained, to despoil such a cherished cricket ground, and all he proposed to do was to take a narrow strip of practice ground, in compensation for which he was prepared to give the club the freehold of 8,000 yards of land near, lease them 4,000 yards and to tunnel beneath the turf so carefully that there would be no interference with play – nay, not a blade of grass would be disturbed. The ire of the club was appeased by the generous nature of the proposal; but the artists remained obdurate, and the Great Northern persisted in their antagonism. Sir Edward Watkin did everything in his power to propitiate the forces still against him. He was willing to raise the question of the agreement with the Great Northern when the line was completed. He was not averse even to the alternative site for the terminus. But his diplomatic elasticity was in vain. The Select Committee, after 28 sittings, found the preamble to the Bill not proved.

The cost of the Parliamentary proceedings was exceedingly heavy, and some of the shareholders became uneasy as to the amount they would be called upon to pay, though they were scarcely so flustered as certain proprietors of the South Eastern Railway, for instance, who were once startled by the discovery that "the solicitor's bill contained 10,000 folios, had occupied 12 months in taxing before the master, and amounted to £240,000".

Sir Edward was not disheartened. He told the shareholders in July 1891, that all the railway decisions given during the session had certainly been curious. But, with a touch of defiance, the directors were a stolid class of men who did not know when they were beaten, convinced as they were travelling on the right line in the interests of 13,000 shareholders, and they proposed to go forward with the Bill in the following session. Some of the cricketers now took alarm again; and at a meeting at Marylebone Cricket Club, Mr Denzil Onslow moved that the Bill should be opposed at every stage of its progress, inasmuch as he believed that the parting of any portion of the freehold at Lord's for the purposes of the railway would be fraught with greatest danger to the interests of cricket. The Resolution was rejected, however, by a majority of members, Sir Henry James reminding the club that the company's proposals were very fair and that they really had no locus standi in opposing the passage of the Bill.

W G Grace was very annoyed when Watkin opted to build his MS&LR line directly beneath the hallowed pitches of Lord's. But Watkin placated his opponents with a gift of land and, as seen here, Firbank used the 'cut and cover' method to build the tunnels across the cricket ground. As promised, the job was finished during the winter. (*LLRRO*)

The MS&LR diverged from the Met at Canfield Place, and Firbank built the above tunnels to emerge at the new terminus at Marylebone station. It was a difficult contract, in having to cross the LNWR main line and the Regent's Canal, as well as avoiding any damage to the Hampstead Baths and Lord's Cricket Ground. (*LLRRO*)

This 1890s view of the Met's station at West Hampstead, looking south towards Baker Street, shows Firbank's navvies' preparations, on the right, for the MS&LR tracks emerging from Canfield Place to join the Met. They would initially share these tracks to the north as far as Quainton Road Junction. *(LLRRO)*

The Met signal box and goods yard at West Hampstead around 1897, showing the completed junction with the MS&LR lines from Marylebone and ready for the 1899 opening. This marked the completion of Firbank's work on contract no.7 to build the railway from here to the new terminus and also his work for Liddell & the Met.*(LLRRO)*

West Hampstead station, again in the 1890s, with no.58, a B class version – with minor changes – of the successful A class Met 4-4-2 tank engines. Running, as here, tender-first was not liked by H M Inspectorate and the Met made half-hearted efforts with turntables at Harrow, Rickmansworth and Chesham. But they were later removed. *(LLRRO)*

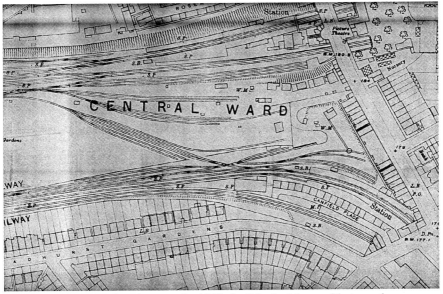

This 1910 map shows major changes. In 1880 the Met had been able to make a connection with the nearby Midland Railway which allowed goods traffic to flow until 1948. Secondly, after the acrimony over sharing the approaches to London, the 'Joint' had been formed, in which the Met provided separate tracks for the GCR to Harrow.

Looking north from Neasden & Kingsbury, the new tracks in the middle have been leased to the GCR for 999 years at £20,000 p.a. The nearer signal box marks the junction with the GW & GC Joint line that could be used to bypass the Met, the threat of which in 1906 led to the Met & GC Joint Committee controlling their shared activities. *(LLRRO)*

When the MS&LR was seeking space for a locomotive depot to serve their new terminus at Marylebone, Watkin sold them some of his surplus land at Neasden. This shows the 6-road engine shed being built around 1898. Robinson's son, Matthew, was to become the Loco Superintendent and occupy an office on the left, beside a large clock. *(LLRRO)*

The grand London terminus of the MS&LR, now the GCR, was at last opened on 9th March 1899. To celebrate the event, a lunch was held in a decorated space between the two island platforms. The President of the Board of Trade congratulated all present and complimented Sir Edward Watkin, probably on extreme right in a wheelchair. *(LLRRO)*

A view across the spacious concourse of Marylebone station, in use, shortly after the opening. The well-stocked W H Smith & Sons bookstall was easily able to cope with the number of passengers, the numbers of which never met the hopes of the GCR. However, this was counter-balanced by the rapid growth in goods traffic with London. *(LOSA)*

Watkin had stipulated that the MS&LR extension to join the Met should be built to the highest standards in order to ensure a smooth passage for his trains. Here on the first day of operation, an up train to Marylebone, headed by a new Pollitt-designed 4-4-0 Class 11A engine no. 859, thunders through Brackley. *(David Jackson Collection)*

The GCR engine shed at Neasden was some 6 miles from Marylebone. In 1903, no.968, a Pollitt 4-2-2 express loco, built for the opening of the line to London, moves off the shed. Neasden, Met, is in the background, with the middle signal box controlling the junction to the GW & GC line and the nearest, that to the GCR shed. *(David Jackson Coll.)*

John George Robinson became the Locomotive Engineer of the GCR in 1900 and introduced an impressive range of engines for them, marked by a combination of elegance and performance. First were the Class 9J 0-6-0 goods engines of 1901, known colloquially as 'Pom-Poms', seen here near Northwood on the Joint. *(David Jackson Coll)*

Later in 1903 came the class 8B express passenger engines, built for the GCR by Beyer-Peacock, with the characteristic attention to flowing lines and to the complementary design of chimney, dome and other features. This down Sheffield express is passing a public crossing near Northwood, one of several on the Joint. *(Frank Cockman Coll.)*

Another Robinson design of 1903 to meet the new demands of the services to London, no.1038 of this class is bound for Marylebone. The elegance of Robinson's engine is nicely matched by the Edwardian dress of the passengers on the platform. *(LOSC)*

In 1903 Robinson also introduced his classic 4-4-2 tank engines for the GCR London suburban services. The C13s were used on the Aylesbury line, whilst the longer range C14s were for the Wycombe route. Here in 1906, a C13 leaves Chesham destined for Marylebone, crossing the Moor for the climb to Chalfont & Latimer. *(R. East Coll.)*

Looking East from Edgware Rd station on the Inner Circle, around 1905. A Met A class tank is entering the station with Oldbury stock, past a multiple electric set in a siding. On the right, the original Met engine shed, before new facilities were built at Neasden. In the background, the fresh competition is manifest by the tower of the new GCR Hotel.*(NRM)*

The ramshackle station at Moor Park remained virtually unchanged from when it was opened in 1910, as Sandy Lodge, to serve the nearby Golf Course. Built entirely of wood, it shook violently whenever a Marylebone express thundered through. This nostalgic photo reveals the strong 'Joint' influence on the primitive facilities. *(LTM)*

The sharing of tracks with the new GCR trains brought home to passengers and the Met that improvements were needed. For example, the original 1867 Beyer-Peacock Class A/B engines were still the mainstay, and this picture of a long-serving Met driver at the controls, unprotected by any cab from the elements, shows the disparity. *(Getty Images)*

The inhabitants of Marylebone, after the club had been propitiated, decided at a meeting held in January 1892 to oppose the project on the ground that the railway would disturb the patients at the Samaritan Free Hospital and in Queen Charlotte's Hospital and, worse still, would dislodge 25,000 persons of the humbler classes from the neighbourhood. Sir Edward Watkin, however went on with his scheme undismayed and was able, at a meeting of shareholders at Manchester in the same month to state that satisfactory arrangements had been made with those who at one time were opponents. Lord's were perfectly satisfied, they had come to a fair understanding with many of the landowners, and they had made a settlement with the Great Northern Company, under which there would be a general interchange of running powers and facilities. The Hon. Baronet, jaunty and sanguine, now thought there was strong probability of getting the Bill through, and believed they might look forward with confidence to the new portion of their line paying 6%.

The Bill came before the Committee of the House on March 21, 1892. The opposition was less formidable; but the promoters, ready for any emergency, were prepared with 159 witnesses. It was explained that the old agreement with the GNR had been superseded by a working arrangement encouraging friendly and reasonable competition over each other's lines, and that the GNR were no longer antagonistic to the new line. Peace, it was also stated, had been made with Lord's Cricket Ground, and some other opponents had been converted into friends. In London the line would begin with a junction close to West Hampstead Station on the Metropolitan Railway and terminate in the Marylebone Road. The station would be fronted by a fine hotel, and at each side would be a 60-ft road giving access to the passenger platforms. A separate entrance would be provided to the goods station and a coal yard would be near the Portman Market, where no objection could be taken to it. For a considerable distance in London the line would be in tunnel, but the company was prepared to pledge not to build over the tunnel and something like 15 acres of land might be converted into some sort of boulevard.

The London County Council still looked askance at the project; and the Art Colony in St John's Wood reiterated their dislike of the line ....Mr Alma Tadema protested against the railway invasion, and maintained that the shake of traffic would interfere with good work; that when the artist sought to put a straight line on the canvas the line would be crooked. Another painter, residing in West Hampstead, said, in sardonic vein, that the new railway would give his neighbours a very good idea of what an earthquake was like, the only difference being that while a natural earthquake was soon over, the earthquake Sir Edward Watkin proposed to work would be continuous.

Mr Bidder, QC, who held a brief for all the opponents, must have had an intuitive misgiving that the opposition was likely to be in vain, for he addressed the Committee in a remarkable speech, declaring that the object of the Bill was not to accommodate the towns and villages on the route of the proposed new line, but to satisfy the ambition of the promoters to become a great trunk line to London. It was, he said meaningly, to accomplish the deep-laid ambitious plans of one man – a man well known in the railway world – whose hope and dream was to terminate his life by running a through carriage from the North to London, and from London to Paris. The Channel Tunnel was part and parcel of Sir Edward Watkin's dream; and he was now leading forward the shareholders of the MS&LR to ruin in the wild belief that this great line would increase their dividends. Mr Littler, QC, for the promoters, held that there was no better pioneer and guide in railway matters than Sir Edward Watkin, and bluntly characterised Mr Bidder's utterances as "rubbish, and highly absurd". These speeches were made on April 18th. On the same day, the Committee having deliberated in private for half an hour, declared the preamble passed!"

In practice, the 51 acres were mainly overcrowded and unhealthy tenements housing about 4,500 of 'labouring families', most of whom were re-housed, including some 2,690 into new blocks built by Firbank's for the GCR as Wharncliffe Gardens, with a school and vicarage. Not a day's play was lost at Lord's!

However, this somewhat cynical excerpt above does give some idea of the complexity and cost of the fight that Watkin had to build Marylebone. We must remember that at the same time he also had to deal with other projects crucial to his grand scheme of things which were in great difficulties. His tunnel being bored under the Channel had reached about 2,000 yards from each shore and yet was obstructed by the British Government, fearing a French invasion. The deep-seated nature of his concern was indicated recently when it was revealed that even in 1975 the British government considered placing a nuclear device in the forthcoming Channel Tunnel in order to be able to block it, if needed. There was also his Tower at Wembley, intended to eclipse that by Eiffel, but now moribund and in addition, the practical aspects of the rail link between the MS&LR and the Met were proving increasingly troublesome. The cost of the latter was also escalating to the extent that hire purchase was being considered to obtain the rolling stock for operating the new line. Relations between the General Managers, William Pollitt (MS&LR) and John Bell (Met) were deteriorating in view of a possible merger between the two railways that would cost one of them his job. Indeed, they were even resisting Watkin's wish for a link at Marylebone to enable the MS&LR trains to join the Met west of Baker Street beyond and thus access the SER – and the Channel Tunnel.

In retrospect, it seems understandable that these and the numerous pressures of Watkin's many other commitments should take their toll on his health. So, although he survived to see the first train, carrying the suitably imposing name of 'The Great Central Railway', depart on 9th March 1899 with suitable celebrations from an appropriately extravagant Marylebone, it was as a passive figure confined to a wheelchair, following his first stroke in 1894. At that time he had resigned all his chairmanships, and when he later died in 1901 the City responded unkindly by marking up the relevant shares in his old companies.

ooooo0000oooooo

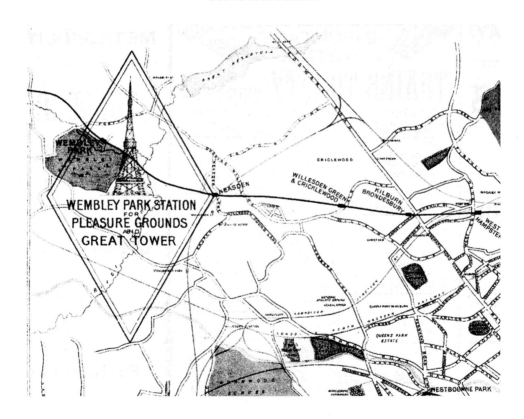

The optimistic inclusion of the Watkin Tower, set in the Wembley Pleasure Gardens, in a Met map of the 1890s.

CHAPTER 6

MARRIAGE À LA MODE

Watkin died in 1901, latterly having played no active role in the control of his fragmenting former empire. Indeed, since his first stroke, his grip on day-to-day decisions had gradually weakened. In particular, he seemed unable to resolve the rift between the MS&LR and the Met over sharing the tracks from the North to London. An obvious solution was to combine the two companies, but William Pollitt and John Bell, respective General Managers of the two lines, fiercely resisted it. As might be expected, both realised that only one could be chosen to lead a merged railway that was being considered by the Boards and, to add 'fuel to the fire', they had been in competition before when both were working as clerks in the same office at the MS&LR. Pollitt saw himself as the manager of a major railway company – not a minor player as he regarded the Met to be – whilst on the other hand, Bell regarded his company as profitable, compared with the GCR which was verging on bankruptcy.

Both viewed any decision on potential capital expenditure, staffing and operation relating to the forced sharing of the line between the southern end of the GCR at Quainton Road and London in the light of how it would affect their own authority. Undoubtedly, this was exacerbated by the initial principles that Watkin had laid down in 1890 on profit sharing (MS&LR having 2/3 and the Met 1/3 part, relating to mileage). This was further aggravated by the lavish plans for a new terminus at Marylebone with a link to the Met and the south coast. Bell tried to enhance the Met position, firstly by using Liddell's early plans to push the Met north to Moreton Pinkney, thereby reducing the MS&LR mileage used to calculate the revenue split and improving his share of profits. Secondly, he restricted MS&LR access to stations close to London. And lastly, he used every decision, from the siting of engine sheds to use of telegraph bell-codes, as reasons to prevaricate and provoke! Pollitt and Bell almost relished their adversarial conflict and had an equal ability to vex with provocative daily hand-delivered letters and barrages of legal attacks, but Pollitt's masterstroke was to start to collaborate with that old enemy of the Met, the GWR!

For some time the GWR had been seeking to shorten their existing route to Birmingham, which was via Oxford, in order to compete effectively with the LNWR, whose slogan was *"London to Birmingham in 2 hours!"* Therefore, in 1897, they began to plan a 'cut-off' route from their existing mainline near Acton to their branch from Maidenhead to High Wycombe. Realising that Watkin's grasp of the

MS&LR and Met was weakening, the GWR was able to encourage the MS&LR (by means of lending capital to the impoverished company) to build a link from their northern main line to Banbury, to improve access to the north. On the basis of this improving relationship, it became apparent to both that a joint approach would both solve the GWR's need for a better Birmingham link, and would offer a way for the MS&LR (now, the imposing Great Central Railway) to bypass the troublesome Met to reach their new terminus at Marylebone. The mutual deterioration of the relationship with the Met reached a peak in 1899, when Pollitt tried to force through a GCR coal train via Aylesbury and the GWR line to London. This provoked Bell to appear personally at the Quainton Road Met signal box and to force it to reverse, an action which only served to encourage the formation of the GW & GC Joint Committee Line. This agreed in 1898 that:

1) The GCR would build a line from Marylebone to Northolt Junction, to which the GWR would build a line from Acton.
2) Their Joint Committee would build a line onwards to High Wycombe and take over the GWR route to Princes Risborough.
3) Their Joint Committee would construct a new line 9 miles north to Ashendon Junction, to form part of the new GWR line to Birmingham and access the GCR main line near Calvert.

As might be expected, Bell took legal action but, in a convoluted judgement, the GCR was allowed to proceed and the implications caused the Met to mollify its confrontational attitude – to some extent! In consequence, Marylebone opened on 9th March 1899, with appropriate pomp, to GCR traffic from the north over the Met tracks as far as Canfield Place. Soon afterwards both Bell and Pollitt retired from the fray, but their enmity lingered on, particularly in the operating and financial areas. The major bones of contention, which continue even today, related firstly to the split of revenues over the shared routes, and secondly to the interlacing of the GCR long-distance fast trains and the Met suburban traffic. The latter was a cause of increasing complaint by the Met, with reports of excessive GCR speeds and their poor timekeeping on entering Met territory. On the GCR side, their frustration with the Met's stubbornness led them to collaborate with the GWR on building the new line which would allow them to bypass the Met, as part of giving the GWR a shorter route to Birmingham.

This continuing quarrel between the Met and the GCR reached a tragic climax with the Aylesbury Railway Disaster on 23rd December 1904. The traditional GCR early morning newspaper and mail train had departed from Marylebone at 2.45 am and was seen by the signalman to pass Canfield Place at speed, in a mist. It was due at Sheffield at 6.20 am, but at 3.40 am the train left the rails on the approach to Aylesbury station, hurling the engine across one platform and all the

Although Watkin had persevered with his Channel Tunnel against determined opposition from the British Army, who feared it would be used by invaders, in the end he was forced to stop excavations. This shows his tunnel through the chalk, still dry when discovered during boring for the recent successful Channel Tunnel project. *(Nick Catford)*

A picture that symbolises the loss of Watkin's power. In the foreground, a line is being built by his own GCR to link to their joint line with his old enemy, the GWR. This would enable them to bypass the Met, which lays over the embankment, behind Watkin's unfinished Wembley Tower - which was intended to eclipse that by Eiffel! *(LLRRO)*

This disastrous crash at Aylesbury on 23rd December 1904, when a GCR express derailed on entering the station, was primarily due to excess speed over a reverse curve. But it reflected a deeper conflict between the Met and the GCR over sharing the tracks between Harrow and Quainton, and forced them into a formal joint operation. *(CfBS)*

Many other problems existed at Aylesbury station as it was shared by the GWR, Met and GCR who all had a history of disagreements. In 1906, it formally came under the control of the two joint committees, with responsibility rotating on a 4-year cycle! Nevertheless, as this collision by a Churchward tank engine illustrates, troubles continued. *(CfBS)*

carriages over the rest of the station, completely blocking it. Into this chaos, the 10.20 pm express bound for Marylebone was rapidly approaching. Although the signalman gave prompt warning of the impending crash ahead and the driver applied the brakes, it was too late and the northern train was still moving when it hit the wreckage. Local people, including the Met staff, rushed to the aid of the scalded crew and injured passengers but both the driver, fireman and two other GCR staff on board the first train died. The primary cause was deemed to be the excessive speed of the driver when entering the sharp reverse bend where the Met joined the GWR into Aylesbury station. But it was apparent to all that it was really the culmination of many problems generated by the grudging attitude of both parties to sharing the same line from London. Sadly, it took this tragedy to bring both companies to their senses. However, Arthur Henderson, an astute financier who had put the GCR's monetary affairs on a sounder footing after the excesses of Watkin, was now Chairman, and he was now able to replace Pollitt with the positive Sam Fay in 1901. Equally, after an interregnum with the brother-in-law of Watkin, the Chairmanship of the Met passed to the future Lord Aberconway, who similarly recruited a new Secretary (and soon General Manager), Robert Selbie. In many ways these two fresh key players, Fay of the GCR and Selbie of the Met, had similar outlooks – they were astute managers, commercially orientated and prepared to judge any issue on its merits.

Against this new background, and spurred on by the Aylesbury disaster, negotiations started in 1905 to come to a formal Agreement to share the route. This covered from Canfield Place, at the approaches to Marylebone and Baker Street, through Harrow to Quainton Road (where the lines again diverged), and including the branches to Chesham, Brill and Verney Junction, but excluding the new Uxbridge branch. It was to be achieved by the Met building parallel tracks from the GCR line at Canfield Place to south of Harrow and leasing them to the GCR. Thus they had unrestricted access to the Joint Line, but were prevented from carrying passengers to any intermediate point without the consent of the Met! North from Harrow, the $48^{1}/_{2}$ miles of the existing Met line were to be under the control of a Met & GC Joint Committee. This Agreement formally came into effect on 2nd of April 1906 on the basis that all costs, capital expenditure and revenues would be shared between the Met and GCR. But as neither side really trusted the other, all management, financial matters, provision of services and staff recruitment would be rotated between the two companies! My earlier books give more details of 'The Agreement' and its initial, somewhat ludicrous, implementation. However, some of these convoluted practices were later modified in the light of their obvious inefficiency (i.e. sending parcels via Baker Street or Marylebone on alternate days), but some remained until recently, such as responsibility for track maintenance being split between north and south of Great Missenden. Working practices also remained strongly influenced by the 'Poggy' men of the GCR and Met old timers, who 'may have buried the hatchet – but well remembered the spot'. The Met management archives reveal many, many lengthy disputes at official levels over whether either party would pay their share of expenditure, such as a bill of £6 for the replacement of one fence post near Rickmansworth, which oscillated for months between the two companies. And similar antagonism could exist at working grades where some would only speak to someone of the other company through a third party!

However, from then onwards there was to be an uneasy truce between the partners in the Joint Committee, but the actions preceding the Agreement, the nature of it, and how it was implemented, significantly constrained the evolution of the Extension – and therefore Metro-land – and continues to have an influence, even today.

oooooOOOOOooooo

Stamps of the Met and Joint Committees: left to right – Metropolitan Railway; Metropolitan & G.C. Joint Committee (1906); Metropolitan & L.N.E.R. Joint Committee (1925), controlling the Watford branch.

CHAPTER 7

THE SEEDS OF METRO-LAND

From the 1840s, a growing number of prominent citizens became concerned about the overcrowding of London, with the consequent growth in squalor and ill health, due to the concentration of labour to support the thriving industrial revolution. Charles Pearson, Solicitor to the City of London, who was the prime mover behind the proposals for what was to become the Metropolitan Railway to ease movement in Central London, also suggested that estates of some 10,000 cottages should be built a few miles down the line to house craftsmen and clerks from the City. He also envisaged that their rents would be reduced by 2d a day to compensate for the cost of their railway ticket to work – a foretaste of a 'London weighting allowance'?

By 1868 Watkin, already Chairman of the SER, had introduced workmen's trains and said: *"Let us find the wealth of London ready to grapple with this great evil of crowding out of the working man. Let us see the capital raised at 5% to build workingmen's houses for 100,000 in any healthy place down our line and we shall be ready........... to carry the people at times that suit them and at prices no greater than the differences in rent and taxes between unhealthy London and the healthy fields beyond"*. In spite of similar altruistic statements, he and other railway leaders did little to alleviate the situation, possibly because it was thought that cheap housing might 'drive out the richer class, who are the more profitable customers'. However, these same pressures were now making it difficult for railways themselves to expand and retain their own workers and artisans for operating their trains. Indeed, Watkin argued that railways should be allowed *"to build little colonies in places contiguous to their railways"* and in 1874 built some houses in isolated places for his local MS&LR staff. Later in the early 1880s, now as Chairman of the Met, he created a 'Neasden Village' estate beside the new locomotive works and sheds for his employees – noting that, in spite of the expense, it would attract *"a better class of workman"*. The estate eventually consisted of some 142 houses in Quainton, Verney and Aylesbury Streets with shops, a school, 2 missions and a St Saviour's Church. There seems little doubt that, with the first train departing at 5.15 am and the last returning at 1.15 am, and his employees working 58 hours or more a week, this was a good investment in his men, apart from the $6^{1}/_{2}$ % return he got in rent.

Around 1882, this was followed by a small development of residential housing near Willesden Green, but the railway at this time was still not really proactive in

The seeds of Metro-land. Top: This 1906 picture shows how the Finchley Road area was still in open countryside.*(LTM)* Middle: Equally, this photo of Watkin's first houses at Neasden for the workers at his new locomotive and carriage works shows how necessary they were to attract and retain staff. *(Brent Archive)* Bottom: Today, those same 'cottages' on the Met Neasden Village Estate. *(LTM)*

Uxbridge had for some time been an attractive target for railway companies in its own right, but the Met also saw it as a route capable of attracting much commuting traffic. Although delayed by disputes with James Staats Forbes of the MDR, this picture shows work on constructing their electric railway from Harrow in about 1902. *(NMSI)*

Watkin had shown an early interest in electrification in order to reduce the worsening problems with smoke in the Inner Circle. This led to the Uxbridge branch being built with electric traction in mind. Originally, there was only one intermediate station on the branch at Ruislip, seen here in 1902, whilst under construction. *(NMSI)*

creating his *"contiguous colonies beside the railway"* to attract passengers. However, Watkin had already unwittingly sown the seeds for the subsequent housing development by the Met that was to be exploited dramatically later. It was in his character to secure any land that might give him room to manoeuvre or negotiate a way of achieving his long-term railway plans, such as his abortive link from Chesham to Tring on the LNWR. Where such projects were subsequently blocked by Parliament, this also created surplus land. Equally, Warkin's grandiose inclinations led to his acquiring space for subsequent double or quadruple tracks with appropriate depots and matching facilities. In these ways, the Met had acquired a large amount of spare land adjacent to its lines. Fortunately, however, as a result of his combative and litigious nature, Watkin had also earlier overcome the statutory restrictions on the Met to develop their own land which, as with other railways had been limited to use 'for the purposes of the undertaking' i.e. strictly railways. For, as a result of the earlier City anxieties over the problems of the Met completing the Circle Line, he was able to get legislation under an Act of 1874 uniquely to allow the Met to exploit its surplus land for other purposes. Thus, these factors of land and the power to develop it became the seeds of Metro-land.

By 1885 the Met had about a thousand tenants in the Willesden and Neasden area, generating about £80,000 p.a., which significantly boosted the Met's profits. Unusually, Watkin felt uneasy that this was mixed into the overall accounts, which clouded his arguments about fares, and so in 1886 he gained agreement that such activities would be segregated under a separate 'Surplus Lands' Committee of the Board (the SLC). It is interesting that at that point, the surplus estates were valued at over £2.5 million and by 1898, further legislation specifically allowed the Met, via the SLC, to purchase land and improve, develop and build upon it. This body subsequently became the touchstone for the creation of what became known as Metro-land; based on the catchment area of Watkin's Met Extension through Middlesex, south Hertfordshire and Buckinghamshire

Although Watkin had been concerned about the vulnerability of submerging building development in the Met accounts, in typical fashion he then used this facility to help fund another of his highly speculative personal projects with francophile connotations – namely a Tower at Wembley to at least equal that in Paris. To this end, the SLC bought a 280 acre estate at Wembley Park for such a tower, plus sport and leisure facilities, and joined the Met in injecting funds into an International Tower Construction Co. to build the 1,159 ft high structure (being Watkin, higher than the Eiffel Tower!). Liddell was made a director of the company and he selected a design by Alan Stewart, an assistant of Benjamin Baker, who helped in the supervision of the erection by Heesan & Froude (who had built the Blackpool Tower). By 1896 it had reached a height of 200 ft, but attracted few visitors and construction ceased. After Watkin's death, the huge Firbank foundations began to sink into the unstable clay soil underneath and 'Watkin's Folly' was torn down in 1907. Firbank's foundations had to be demolished by explosives and some 2,700 tons of metal were sold as scrap!

But again, perhaps Watkin had the last laugh, for most of the land was later developed mainly as a large Metro-land housing estate. It also became the site for the very popular British Empire Exhibition in 1924, with its iconic Wembley football stadium – all of which again provided excellent business for the Met for many years to come.

ooooo0000ooooo

Metro-land style publicity for the British Empire Exhibition of 1924-5. This attracted some 27.1 million visitors and subsequent events also provided a steady income for the Met. However, revenue sharing was an ongoing source of acrimony within the Joint.

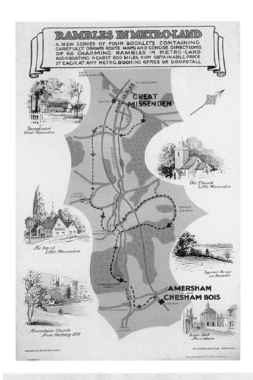

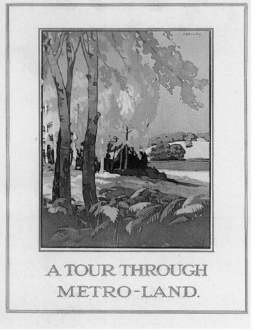

Examples of Met advertising illustrating the varied attractions of Metro-land.

The Met published an annual Metro-land guide for most years from 1916 to 1932. Above are the covers of the 1916 (bottom) and 1926 issues. It proclaimed the Met as the best way to travel around London and see the attractions of the country to the north-west.

The covers of the later Metro-land guides of 1930 (bottom) and 1932. Increasingly, these stressed the advantages of living in Metro-land and acquiring a home on one of the Metropolitan Railway Country Estates sites or many associated developments.

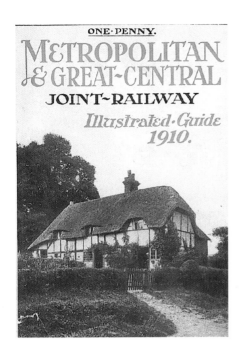

The Joint Committees that actually controlled the operations of the Met beyond Harrow were somewhat restricted in publicising their services. Above are some examples of the few such items issued by them. Top, a Met & GC 1910 guide that was short-lived and right a 1920's advert. Bottom, a 1930 Moor Park poster by the Met & LNER Jt. Cttee.

CHAPTER 8

THE MAKING OF METRO-LAND

Full advantage of these opportunities was to be taken by Robert Selbie, who was appointed Secretary of the Met in 1903 and then General Manager in 1908. Indeed, he soon realised that he had to generate profitable business from Watkin's wildly over-extended Met, in order to make it viable. To achieve this, he saw that the Met had to create a virtuous circle out of attracting more passengers, with better trains and services, by enticing them to visit, commute and live in the area currently served by the Met. By doing this, it would also establish an infrastructure, which would itself generate goods and passenger traffic for the existing railway. His analysis of Met traffic encouraged this strategy for the central London traffic, and revenues were almost static owing to intense competition from the Underground Group and the new bus services. But by contrast, more people were travelling from outside London to work. However, the Met was still desperately short of enough potential business on the Extension, due as pointed out earlier, to the sparsely populated nature of its route through the countryside of Middlesex, Hertfordshire and Buckinghamshire. But Selbie recognised that this could now be turned to advantage by developing the relatively cheap land for a new generation of what we now term commuters.

Selbie was well aware of the advantage of having a readily identifiable label for his concept, having seen the actions of the various deep-level underground tube railways which competed with him in central London. They had banded together under the brand of 'UndergrounD', with a red, white and blue roundel and bar as their common emblem. Thus, the first step was to introduce a distinctive sign on Met stations and this became a red diamond with a blue bar bearing the station name in white lettering. However, elsewhere, other brands such as Cadbury, Co-op, Beecham and Colman were being promoted as having implications wider than a specific product in order to evoke a greater sense of well-being and confidence – and so **Metro-land** was born.

It is uncertain when the expression 'Metro-land' was devised. One of the first examples of its use is in a poem by George Sims (whose most famous work was *'A Christmas Day in the Workhouse'*). The beginning of this poem is given on the title page of this book and the rest is as follows:

"Metro-land, Metro-land,
Leafy dell and woodland fair,
Land of love and hope and peace,
Land where all your troubles cease,
Metro-land, Metro-land,
Waft, O waft me there.
Hearts are lighter, eyes are brighter,
In Metro-land, Metro-land."

The able John Wardle, who had worked for Watkin on the Grand Trunk Railway of Canada, was recruited by Selbie and appointed Commercial Manager of the Met in 1908, and he subsequently claimed to have devised the expression. However, so did one of his copywriters, a James Garland, but certainly the Met first applied it in 1915 and began to use Metro-land on reprints of the publications and pamphlets that were already in existence. Later, Wardle promoted the word 'Metro' as shorthand for the Met in London – or the metropolis – even having connotations of the Paris Metro, with whom the Met kept in touch. Although Selbie had doubts, Wardle persisted with 'Metro' from 1920 and last used it during the opening of the Stanmore branch in 1932.

As in the poem by Sims, the initial spelling of Metro-land was hyphenated but subsequently every variation was used as it came into general use, often in a slightly rustic typeface. Soon Metro-land was widely deployed to encourage passengers to use the Met, and preferably become residents. The Commercial Department's advertising aimed to create the impression that Metro-land was a way of life in sylvan surroundings by using a simple, artless language that resonated with those seeking a new life outside London. Classic examples were:

"prim towns set amongst well-timbered and watered countryside"
"a beautiful and unspoilt unknown rural Arcadia"
"a good piece of English soil in which to build a home and strike root"
"the good air of the Chilterns invites health by day and sleep by night"

The Commercial Department of the Met was already active with traditional posters and was even making an early silent film in 1910 of the Extension route, taken from the front of a moving train, which provides a fascinating glimpse of the still open countryside near London. But in 1915 the Department began their campaign centred on Metro-land. New-style posters were the main thrust, promulgating the sentiments of Metro-land, with maps where distances were distorted in order to favour the proximity of Metro-land to London, and which highlighted the ready availability of golf courses and hunting. A continuing series of guides was issued of picturesque routes ('with invigorating exercise') to encourage visitors, ramblers and cyclists to use the Met to explore Metro-land and hopefully, to live there. Relevant books and postcards were part of the campaigns, coupled to char-a-banc tours covering some 45 miles for 25p. The annual Metro-land guide was intended to attract home-seekers, by skilfully encapsulating advertisements within an attractive description of the idyllic allures of the countryside traversed by the Met. This was complemented by publications such as *Homes in Metro-land* and *Where to Live* which were a harder sell of specific properties. All these marketing activities were united by a consistent style of presentation and were intended to conjure up the availability of an almost Utopian environment offering a peaceful, quiet, civilised home as a refuge from the daily grind of work. Indeed they subtly suggested a setting that could be melded to meet everyone's desires.

The nature of the publicity that Wardle organised for Metro-land was, by today's standards, somewhat simplistic, naïve and sentimental, but in some ways it was striking in its directness, intent on rousing the latent desires discussed in the next Chapter. Apart from the inevitable element of nostalgia when taken up in the memorable poems by Sir John Betjeman, the word Metro-land now had a life of its own – being used in songs like *My little Metro-land home*, the style of which is indicated by the mawkish concluding lines –

> — *"it's a very short distance by rail on the Met
> and at the gate you'll find waiting, sweet Violet"*

Metro-land was even used as a surname for characters in books by Baroness Orczy and Evelyn Waugh, whilst more recently Julian Barnes employed it as the title of a reflective novel. All this has led to Metro-land becoming embedded in our language as being associated with the ambience of 'middle England'.

Selbie had already started on his push to revitalise the Met by visiting the USA to study railway electrification and now, as General Manager, he was given free rein to introduce modernisation and more efficient working practices orientated towards greater passenger satisfaction. Nevertheless, these had to be implemented against the background of the severe financial stringency resulting from the excesses of the Watkin era. It is indicative that amongst the staff, the Met was known as the "skilled with **scrap and** know lady **luck**" railway!

In addition, the ramifications of the past bruising disagreements with the GCR restricted Selbie. Firstly, the GW & GC Joint line – created out of frustration by the GCR – had effectively blocked any expansion of the Met into the prosperous area of south Bucks, whereas the Met had earlier seriously considered routing the Extension from the then end of the line at Rickmansworth to High Wycombe. The matter arose again in 1892, when Bell commissioned a survey of a possible branch from Rickmansworth to High Wycombe. A consultant engineer, J Wolf Barry, proposed a 12 mile long branch, either a more northerly line via Chalfont St Giles with a tunnel over 2,000 yards long into High Wycombe, or to the south through Chalfont St Peter and Beaconsfield. The Met Board rejected the plans in 1896, on the grounds of cost in the case of the former route, and problematic land ownership with regard to the latter. But the activity again only served to annoy the GWR! As if in retaliation, in later years the GW & GC Joint began to develop their territory along the lines of Metro-land. Not as well, or intensively, but benefiting from the synergy with the obvious success of Metro-land. Equally, to the north, the main LNWR line through Harrow and Watford hemmed in the Met, although later Selbie created branches to Watford and Stanmore, and even considered extending the former to St Albans.

Secondly, the Met now had to operate their Extension in agreement with the GCR, who were reluctant to invest their own limited capital in improvement schemes in which they felt the Met would be the main beneficiary. In later years, the GCR also became concerned that further weakening of their finances would prejudice their status in the inevitable merger into what was to become the London & North Eastern Railway in 1923.

However, the Met's publicity activities were to some extent augmented by the parallel operations of the GCR/LNER and the Joint. As mentioned earlier, the LNER were also somewhat lukewarm about bolstering Metro-land in view of their reservations about the costs implicit in the Met expansion plans over the Joint. Equally, the Joint itself was heavily restricted, by the terms of the 1906 Agreement to only advertising within Joint territory and for 'local' traffic. Indeed, the only Joint guides appeared in 1906 and 1908, followed by some walker's guides, and a few examples of such collaboration are given in this book. Avoiding the issue, the LNER tended to advertise 'the Chilterns' in general, with rambling and other publications which would also benefit their other route from Marylebone via Northolt, Beaconsfield and High Wycombe

Selbie also had to acknowledge that the GCR, as a result of the efforts of their outstanding Chief Engineer John G Robinson, had equipped the new route to London with a fleet of excellent locomotives and rolling stock. Passengers on the Joint were thus easily able to compare these with the venerable Met stock, which had originated many years ago on the original underground system. Selbie was deluged with complaints from Met travellers, but in retrospect, this competitive pressure from the perceived superior quality of the GCR services ('rapid travel in luxury') seems to have reinforced Selbie's plans to improve his own trains. In attempting to reach parity with GCR services over the Joint, he had to recognise that he ran a much smaller company (the Met was about an $1/8$ of the size of the GCR), with correspondingly fewer physical and financial resources. For example, whilst Robinson had the backing of a full-scale locomotive manufacturing facility for the GCR at Gorton, his opposite number,

Charles Jones, at the Met works at Neasden, had relatively few facilities and relied on outside suppliers to a major extent. However, Selbie had energy, common sense and commercial acumen, combined with an attention to detail that permeated the Met – often to the disquiet of lowly clerks and workers. By effectively harnessing his meagre resources, he was able to create a 'good little 'un'. He also felt that to stop capital expenditure was never the right response to hard times and he continued to seek long-term improvements in the Met, even during the precarious financial environment of the First World War and the subsequent Depression.

Selbie believed that the key to creating the impression amongst potential commuters of a supportive, capable and trustworthy service was to provide the full spectrum of facilities, matching his larger main line competitors. This image of a 'real' railway also gave status to Selbie in the inevitable contemporary wrangling over rationalisation of the surface and underground railway networks, following the period of Government control during the 1914-18 war. However, the 'trust' that the Met really wanted was in convincing potential homebuyers that they could put their faith in the type of housing available in Metro-land and spend the rest of their commuting lives travelling on the railway. This point about confidence in the homes was a strong argument for, in the post-war explosion of speculative building, some construction quality standards had fallen so badly that such homes became colloquially known as 'jerry-built'.

Whilst Selbie remained conscious of the need to create an image of Metro-land in order to bring in more traffic and utilise the fragile route that Watkin had built, he also realised that the Met had to be brought up to a competitive operational standard. This involved a prudent and measured investment in infrastructure and trains. He saw little merit in expanding the Met routes while the existing Extension still had excess capacity, with the exception of a branch to the potentially lucrative town of Watford. Plans were soon made for such a line and land began to be acquired. In view of the success of the electrified line to Uxbridge, it was also envisaged that the Watford branch would be included in electrification from Harrow to Rickmansworth. The main track work was to be the provision of four lines from Finchley Road to Wembley Park to ease the congestion nearing London.

The other aspect of improving the Met infrastructure was an upgrade by their architect, C W Clarke, of most existing stations and the construction of some new ones. This culminated in an imposing headquarters and Chiltern Court luxury flats built at Baker Street station, costing some £500,000, yet yielding over £40,000 p.a., including *ground* rent for flats built *over* the railway lines! These and other new facilities were complementary to a range of new services intended to meet the rising expectations of Metro-landers and match the main line standards of the GCR also working the Joint. Selbie steadily introduced better freight and goods facilities, from the more esoteric vans for hunting horses, to the mundane, but profitable,

The Met Uxbridge branch opened in 1904, but delays with the electrical equipment meant that the service was initially with steam traction. Here an Uxbridge-bound train is hauled by an early Met Class A 4-4-0T engine No.6, 'Medusa', built in 1864 and now fitted with a cab. In the background is the footbridge that preceded the subway. *(F M Gates Coll.)*

The first Met multiple-electric stock on trial near Neasden, where a new power station had been built near the existing works. This supplied 11kv, 3-phase at 331/3 cycles which was converted to 660v dc. Made by MRCW, with Westinghouse motors, the stock were a mixture of British and American practices, with access via end platforms. *(LLRRO)*

In the light of the experiences with the 1904 multiple-electric stock, those following in 1905-7 had their platform access replaced by sliding doors on the sides. Such a 3-car set is shown at Ickenham Halte, built in 1905 hopefully to serve new Met estates. It was only a basic wooden structure and acted as a collecting point for milk churns. *(LLRRO)*

Looking north at Harrow-on-the-Hill station following electrification. A subway has now replaced the footbridge and sidings have been provided on the extreme right to facilitate the change-over from electric to steam traction for the Met trains travelling over the Joint lines to Bucks. *(LOSC)*

The Met now required electric locomotives to haul the coaches of the longer-distance steam trains over the newly electrified sections and the Inner Circle. The first were delivered to Neasden in 1905 from MRCW, with electrical equipment from Westinghouse, to a specification by Thomas Parker, consultant to the Met. *(teckytony/tubeprune)*. Initially there were many electrical problems with the so-called 'camel backs', but the main difficulty continued to be the drivers' position, such that the visibility from his cab was poor. *(Getty Images)*

Learning from the experience with the Westinghouse 'camel-backs', in 1906 the Met obtained some new electric locomotives, to an improved design from BT-H, with the bodies from Neasden and MRCW. Retaining the Bo-Bo wheel arrangement, no.11 is pictured here during initial trials and required no major modifications. *(IEE)*

The 1905 multiple-electric cars were very successful, except that entry and exit were poor compared with compartment stock. A programme of modification with more sliding doors was started in 1911, but delayed by the First World War. A wartime female guard gives the 'away' at Neasden, whilst behind the milk churns await. *(Getty Images)*

Further new multiple-electric cars were introduced in 1913 to cope with the demands of the East London and Uxbridge branches. These were interchangeable with the 1905 stock and often worked in a mixed formation. Here, one of the 1913 driving cars is seen undergoing work on its BTH/GEC motor bogies at Neasden works. *(H C Casserley)*

Incredibly, at the same time as the top picture, the venerable Met steam engine Class A 4-4-0 tank no.33 built in 1868 was also undergoing major repairs at Neasden works. This contrast highlights Selbie's pressing need for the Met to develop an adequate range of steam locomotives to cope with the increasing demands of Metro-land. *(H C Casserley)*

In 1920, the H Class of 4-4-4T engines were obtained from Kerr Stuart to a Met design. Mainly used on passenger trains, they were capable of good acceleration and their flexible wheelbase could cope with the Chesham branch curves. In 1931, no.106 is passing through Chorleywood, where this type was once recorded at 75mph. *(Gamble/Carpenter)*

Selbie wanted some more powerful freight engines and in 1925, the K class 2-6-4Ts were built by Armstrong-Whitworth, using ex-WD parts of a Maunsell design. They were capable of pulling some 600 tons at 35 mph. Here, an up freight at Chorleywood in 1931 hauled by No.111 is from the Verney Junction exchange sidings. *(Gamble/Carpenter)*

To establish the status of the Met in the minds of potential Metro-landers and to compete with the GCR, they introduced two Pullman cars in 1910, 'Mayflower' and 'Galatea'. These served 5 trains daily to and from Amersham, Chesham, Aylesbury and Verney Junction. Their ambience can be judged by this picture, looking towards the bar. *(LTM)*

Verney Junction, Watkin's 'Clapham Junction', never matched his expectations. In 1939, on the right, an elegant Met H class loco no.103 with Dreadnought coaches and Pullman (for a 10p supplement) wait for the return trip to London. On the LMS line, an ex-Bletchley train behind No.6704, heads sedately westwards for Oxford. *(H C Casserley)*

The opening of the Watford branch in 1925 highlighted the Met's need for new multiple-electric stock with higher speeds for the longer Metro-land trips. Over the next few years, a number of variants of the highly successful T stock were brought into service. Above, some are prepared at Wembley for the 1933 Cup Final specials. *(Getty Images)*

A 1930s view from Wembley Park, looking south towards Neasden. In the background, the Met power station supplies the predominately electrified tracks. On the left, a set of 1913 stock is passing a Wembley Exhibition platform. In the centre are two trains of Met T stock, whilst to the right, an LNER steam train heads for Aylesbury. *(Foxell/Orbit)*

Increasing traffic also led to consideration of upgrading the earlier Bo-Bo electric locos, but this proved impractical, and new ones were built by Met-Vic, from 1921 onwards. At the new change-over point of Rickmansworth, No.20 is in original condition with brass headlamps, but without nameplates (later 'Sir Christopher Wren'). *(Real Photos)*

The interior of the cab of one of the Met-Vic Bo-Bo electric locomotives. In contrast with the previous types, all the electrical equipment was mounted along the centreline, leaving the controls at each end, although it is doubtful whether it would meet the current safety regulations. At speed, the ride was 'rough' and the ventilation 'more than adequate'.

deliveries of parcels and building materials. Passengers were better catered for with the modern 'Dreadnought' coaches (so called, after the large, stately and powerful Edwardian battleships) and in 1910, with the introduction of two Pullman dining cars – offering breakfast for the City travellers in the morning and a restful G&T at 1/- during the return home from work or after the theatre.

The Met had introduced electric traction on its underground lines, primarily to eliminate the effects of locomotive pollution, and extended it to Harrow and over the new Uxbridge branch in 1905. These sections were worked by multiple-electric stock, or for the Extension, some Westinghouse and BTH electric locomotives to the point for changeover to steam haulage. To complete the transformation, Selbie planned to continue electrification to Rickmansworth and the proposed new branch to Watford, however the First World War brought a halt to these hopes until 1925. But in preparation for these services, new modern T-stock multiple-electric units and the Met's celebrated Metropolitan-Vickers Bo-Bo electric locomotives were ordered.

Recognising that more powerful steam locomotives were necessary to replace the veteran Beyer-Peacock A/B class engines of the 1860s, the Met had also introduced a range of new tank locomotives: the C, D, E, and F classes. But only the few Es and Fs were a complete success, and so even when electrification was implemented, new steam locomotives were needed to cope with the heavier passenger loading and goods traffic. Selbie ordered over 1915-24 such a range of new tank engines, the G mixed-traffic (0-6-2), H passenger (4-4-4) and K (2-6-4) heavy goods classes. These were built by private locomotive suppliers to Met specifications. They combined elegance with utility, the performance necessary to match the acceleration of the Met electric services, and the power to handle heavy trains over the sharp curves and gradients of the Chilterns.

ooooo0000ooooo

CHAPTER 9

THE DESIRE FOR METRO-LAND

We can understand the virtue of Selbie's scheme of offering affordable homes, built on surplus Met lands, in the semi-rural countryside, for potential commuters. Likely buyers could be attracted by the fast and comfortable trains to become regular commuters and thus generate ongoing stable and profitable revenue for the Met. But a question remains: why did so many people actually take such a fundamental step as to move to Metro-land, and turn the implementation into such a success that, in many ways, it outgrew the Met.

As mentioned earlier, Watkin had built an estate for his workers near Neasden Works, which was then in the country on the outskirts of London, but this was primarily in his own interests in attracting them to the Works. Equally, other railway employers, such as the GWR at Swindon, were creating similar housing. Indeed, industry in general had been undertaking like projects such as Saltaire, Port Sunlight and Bournville. These demonstrated that this approach developed a stable, cohesive workforce, with whom improved living conditions reduced sickness and absenteeism, and encouraged training for skills needed by the company. In one sense, these were evolutions of the housing developments often associated with the factories, mines etc. of the industrial revolution, where the accommodation might be 'tied' in some way to the employer. It also reflected a mix of altruistic motives created by the growing social conscience about the appalling living conditions of the majority of workers, and the employers' drive to achieve greater efficiency and to encourage a more compliant workforce. In parallel, the notion of the 'Garden City Suburb', not necessarily linked to one industry, was launched by Ebenezer Howard in his 1898 book, *Tomorrow: The Peaceful Path to Real Reform.* This proposed imaginative planning, giving an ordered variety of layouts, in which architecture was combined pleasantly with its natural background. It was realised first at Letchworth in 1903 and subsequently at Welwyn Garden City and elsewhere.

One of the consequences of the industrial revolution was the improvement in travel and communications – in which railways, with their national telegraph systems, played a vital enabling role – thus widening awareness amongst the general public of the existence of such better living conditions. Just knowing that life could be a bit better created an aspiration that had a cumulative effect as every new generation could compare its opportunities with those of its parents. In parallel, the wealth of the working class was increasing – not perhaps in proportion to that of the wealthy

– but inevitably enough to be able to afford and absorb the growing output of the products of mass production.

By the time of Metro-land, such aspirations for a 'better life' had become a complex amalgam of desires, set against a background of the consequences of overcrowding and pollution and the aftermath of the terrible human losses of the First World War. The latter victory had come at a time of apparent strength of the British Empire and it was easy to accept the politician's view that this had been 'the war to end all wars'. Certainly, after the losses from the war and the subsequent deprivations of an influenza pandemic, which killed as many as the war, people felt that their circumstances deserved to improve. The fact that the Prime Minister, Lloyd George, had promised 'a land fit for heroes' and similar inducements, served to reinforce a general sense of hope and optimism for the future. Obviously, better and stable employment was the priority of the workforce, but after this, having a satisfactory home of one's own was the basic motivation. A common phrase at this time was, 'an Englishman's home is his castle', even if the reality of his domain was to be a shed in the back garden!

Although many had never lived in what they believed was a satisfactory dwelling, most families carried a picture in their mind of an 'ideal home' in 'this green and pleasant land', which was in some way set apart from others and thus clearly identifiable as their own property. Then it should be of superior quality to their existing home, being less crowded, more light and airy, and in a healthier environment – set in a garden, overlooking a rural landscape – representing a better place for the children to grow up in. But beneath these simple idealistic dreams lay complicated solutions for, obviously, Britain was not large enough to accommodate everyone if they each had separate homes built upon this principle, and this would create more social problems than it solved. In practice, people seemed to like living near others so that they had the option of close association – if they so wished – but not too close! In other words, a somewhat controlled environment in which there would be few surprises. From this, constrained by the realities of cost of land, the need to minimise construction costs and to provide roads and services, came the concept of building an estate of homes. Again, balancing the desire for some uniformity in housing with aspirations for upward mobility, suggested that the developer should offer a reasonable range of homes, from cheaper semi-detached to more expensive detached designs, each with a range of options for the number of rooms and size of garden plots. It is interesting that some of the medium-sized houses still included a 'maid's room' and 'serving hatches, soundproofed so that servants cannot hear the conversations', although even in the more affluent homes the trend was now for a 'daily' to assist with the chores. Watkin had established, at his workers' estate at Neasden, the principle that the size of house should be related to the grade of staff. However, later steps were taken to ensure that individual estates were aimed at different markets, but with a price range not so great as to make the best seem completely unobtainable. To give some semblance of individuality to a few basic designs, it was common to make superficial modifications by using various decorative features. Exteriors could be varied with 'pebble-dash', 'mock-Tudor' and similar finishes, whilst names such as 'Dunromyn' and 'Windy Ridge' were given to homes to add a distinctive touch.

A 'country' flavour to the appearance of houses was also often deployed. This reflected the real wish to escape to the countryside and avoid the demonstrable overcrowding and pollution in London. Both were due to the amount of manufacturing industry concentrated in this area, combined with the consumption of large quantities of coal generating noxious smoke. Again, improvements in travel meant that most city dwellers now had the opportunity to see the countryside on day trips and excursions and, on the basis of relatively brief summer experiences they hankered for what seemed to be an idyllic setting. Of course this was untrue, for the effects of weather, isolation and minimal services could be just as disadvantageous in different ways as a city environment. But the potential mover to Metro-land was led to expect a structured, semi-rural environment, in a civilised or tamed countryside: rather like living in a National Park. The concurrent establishment of the Green Belt encouraged that possibility.

The concept of a Green Belt around London can be traced back to when Queen Elizabeth I banned building within 3 miles of the City gates in order to preserve agriculture for food supplies near the town! Later, in 1657, the Commonwealth Parliament only allowed building plots of more than 4 acres within 10 miles of London. But the first definition of the Green Belt came in 1927 from the then Minister of Health, Neville Chamberlain, who decided that 'London should be provided with an agricultural belt to form a dividing line between London, as it is, and the satellites or new developments'. By 1935, the London County Council (LCC) was acquiring land suitable for creating such a buffer and this policy was enshrined in an Act of 1938 giving Government the right to control major developments and secure further land: in effect, defining the perimeter of Metro-land. Looking to the future during the last war, Professor Patrick Abercrombie defined a future plan for London with concentric rings of decreasing building density culminating in a outer country circlet – thus confirming the Green Belt in most people's minds.

For those considering moving to Metro-land, the presence of any industry was to be avoided, or should at least not be visible, and in consequence Metro-land sites often mentioned 'no factory chimneys'. But in contrast, an infrastructure of doctors, shops, main services, roads and railways (for fathers to go to work and mothers to visit the West End shops) was expected to be within easy reach.

So, we have an expectation of a new home set in a small estate, within a reasonable walking distance of a station, near – but not too close – to the homes of people of similar, or slightly higher, status. Whilst most wanted a readily accessible countryside, in practice few actually used it. But at a time when epidemics of influenza, polio and TB were commonplace, the country had important connotations of health, and so height and fresh air were sold as a significant advantage. Thus, Metro-land was highlighted as being 120-900 feet above sea level. The basic desire was for the estate to be set in a tamed landscape, but with all the necessary facilities at hand. Inside the house existed a similar contradiction between the notion of a simple country cottage life and the reality, which in practice involved a lot of manual effort on the part of the wife, and the concept of increased leisure facilitated by new labour-saving equipment, it becoming a mark of status for a wife not to have to work. Out went the coal-fired kitchen range (with its black Zebra polish) for cooking and heating water and in came the Ideal boiler with a separate gas, or perhaps even electric, stove.

The remaining link in the achievement of these aspirations was the crucial one, namely the ability of families to afford such dreams. Firstly, the cost of houses on Metro-land estates was minimised by the relatively low cost of the land, which in the early 1930s was of the order of £175 per acre, and about 10 houses could be built on an acre. Secondly, material prices were falling and labour costs were low. The developers were usually building large estates and could therefore commit themselves to a few similar designs, bulk purchase of materials and fittings, a stable workforce and some mechanisation of construction, all of which also reduced costs. At Harrow Garden Village, Reid's first laid some 5 miles of roads and supplied the materials from a Met siding via their own Decauville narrow gauge railway (ex-WD, used for constructing defences in France during the War). They worked on the basis that a pair of semi-detached houses could be built in three weeks. Thus houses were on sale at £600-£3,000 with a difference between leasehold and freehold of £100-200. The other side of the affordability equation was the question of the availability of the finance to match the optimism of potential buyers. Some houses were rented, as had previously been the common practice for all classes, including the rich, before 1914, but in practice this gap was now bridged by the increasing use of mortgages, which had been facilitated by new legislation in 1923. The builders in effect by underwriting the difference, reduced deposits from 20% to 10%, or even to 5%. In turn, the builders received a Government subsidy of some £75 to support employment in the building suppliers. Now the developers could proudly advertise that their new properties were available for deposits of 10% with repayments over 15 years. Also, the builders were not reticent in mentioning that an early purchase of a house on a new estate was likely to appreciate rapidly in value as the development moved to completion.

ooooo0000ooooo

CHAPTER 10

METRO-LAND GROWS

By 1912, Selbie's first improvements to the Met operations were beginning to bear fruit with an increase in passenger and freight traffic. He now turned his attention to exploiting the opportunities to generate more tied customers in the manner created earlier by Watkin's Surplus Lands Committee (SLC). The popularity of existing housing close to the Met stations was already apparent and estate agents reported a pent-up demand for properties for rent below £100 p.a. But Selbie felt that the arrangements via the SLC did not give the Met sufficient benefit from exploiting this market. He therefore proposed to the Met Board that a distinct company be formed under the Met, which could develop estates alongside the Met lines. Whilst the Board readily agreed in principle, action was suspended as a result of the First World War (1914-18), but Selbie was soon pointing out that 'there will be a large demand for houses as soon as Peace is declared and the Forces are demobilised'. Later the Board agreed his plans for a separate company, Metropolitan Railway Country Estates Ltd (MRCE), in effect controlled and mainly funded by the Met. When MRCE Ltd was floated in January 1919, 'preferential consideration' for the shares was given to Met and SLC shareholders. The favoured treatment of the MRCE continued with the Met providing staff and offices at their Baker Street Headquarters, a wide range of support such as free advertising on their stations, and free first-class rail tickets to attract potential MRCE home buyers.

Whilst this followed naturally from Watkin's much earlier pioneering scheme, Selbie now realised that the new MRCE represented a significant expansion of operations which might bring it back into conflict with the original legislation. After legal advice, he decided to try to avoid any possibility of an outcry by the Met itself not taking any direct financial holding in the MRCE. However it did exert an indirect control by means of a Chairman, key directors and by providing use of Met facilities, such as legal, commercial and publicity departments. This was a very convenient subterfuge, which enabled a somewhat self-satisfied Selbie to comment, 'railway companies are trusted and not open to the suspicion that often attaches to the speculative builder or developer'. Indeed, it could be said that the MRCE's activities also attracted and provided a cloak of respectability for nearby speculative builders – although surely of a better type! However, the MRCE exercised a fair degree of control over the sites it owned: determining the layout of the estate with detailed plans including shops, amenities, etc., and designing and building a number of the first houses to set the appropriate standard. This was supervised by Charles Walter Clark FRIBA, the

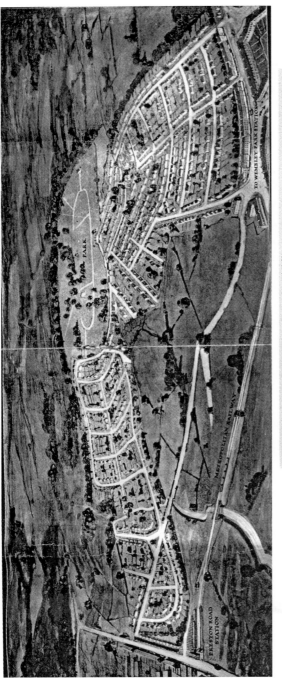

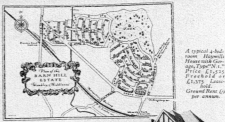

In the 1930s, Barn Hill was used by Haymills as the hub of housing development that, in effect, linked the Met Wembley Park and Preston Road stations. The 'river' featured in the artist's impression is the Wealdstone Brook. *(Brent Archive)*

HARROW GARDEN VILLAGE ESTATE

TYPE "A." Compact semi-detached seven-room residence. Ideal for small family. A marked advance on that obtainable elsewhere. Weekly repayments 28s. 5d. Deposit £50.

PRICE £895 FREEHOLD

TYPE "B." Delightful detached self-contained seven-roomed house. Pleasing and practical elevation, well-proportioned and conveniently arranged rooms, good garden. Weekly repayments 33s. 7d. Deposit £50.

PRICE £1,050 FREEHOLD

TYPICAL REID HOUSE, HARROW GARDEN VILLAGE

A PERSONAL STATEMENT BY E. S. REID

ON the adjoining pages are shown some of the types of houses erected by E. S. Reid and in addition to these there are many other types also to choose from.

From the accompanying plan it will be seen that E. S. Reid's estate has the particular advantage of being **self-contained** and wherever you choose a house on this Estate you may rest assured that you will be surrounded by other of E. S. Reid's houses, and by this it is intended to convey that you may be sure that you will not have a nasty cheap mass production house anywhere near you to lower the value of your own property.

In developing this section (immediately adjoining Rayners Lane Station entrance) **great care has been exercised,** without regard of expense, to keep right away from the monotony of mass production houses which are so swiftly covering the suburbs of London. **It must appeal** to every-one in choosing their house

Continued on page 120.

TYPE "C." Specially large seven-room semi-detached residence. A very popular type of house. Good garden. A house of which you can be justly proud. Weekly repayments 34s. 4d. Deposit £50.

PRICE £1,075 FREEHOLD

TYPE "D." Tudor type seven-room semi-detached house complete with verandah and spacious porch. Without question the finest value obtainable. Weekly repayments 33s. 5d. Deposit £110.

PRICE £1,100 FREEHOLD

E. S. REID

STATION ESTATE OFFICE

HARROW GARDEN VILLAGE
RAYNERS LANE STATION, MIDDLESEX

SAY YOU SAW IT IN "METRO-LAND."

SAY YOU SAW IT IN "METRO-LAND."

Above: Although North Harrow station itself was still a wooden structure, in the early 1930s the entrance had been rebuilt by Clark in the then current cream-tiled style of the Met as a Joint station with a parade of shops. *(LTM)* Top: The nearby Harrow Garden Village estate, built by E S Reid, was the largest of the Metro-land building developments and epitomises the types of houses available in the inter-war years. *(LTM)*

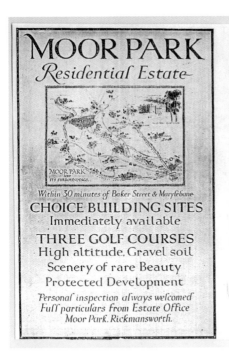

MOOR PARK
Residential Estate

Within 30 minutes of Baker Street & Marylebone

CHOICE BUILDING SITES
Immediately available

THREE GOLF COURSES
High altitude, Gravel soil
Scenery of rare Beauty
Protected Development

*Personal inspection always welcomed
Full particulars from Estate Office
Moor Park, Rickmansworth.*

MOOR PARK
Residential Estate

Beautifully Wooded Heights
PROTECTED
DEVELOPMENT
Three 18 Hole Golf Courses,
Hard & Grass Tennis Courts,
Delightful Country Club.

*Particulars of Choice Freehold Building Sites from
The Estate Office, The Club House, Moor Park
and the Principal Agents.*

The stately home of Lord Ebury at Moor Park was developed as a golf club and Lord Leverhulme's property company used it as a focus for building an estate of superior detached houses. It was served by a wooden station called Sandy Lodge, built in 1910 to serve the Golf Course, becoming Moor Park & Sandy Lodge station in 1923.

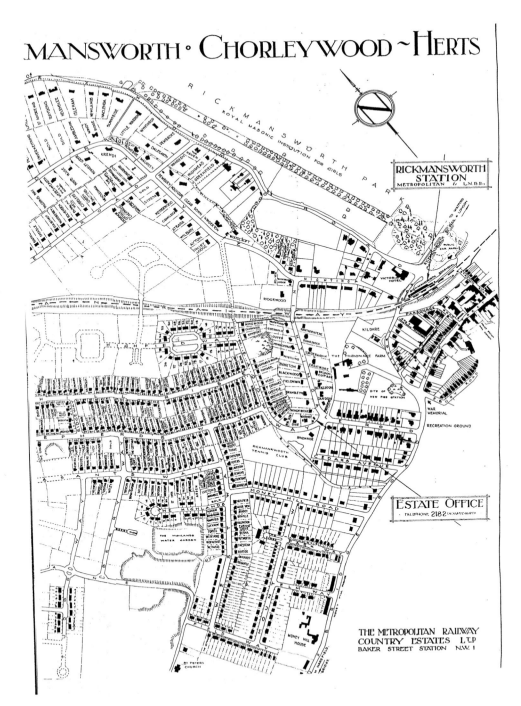

Map of part of the Cedars Estate, near Rickmansworth, from the MRCE brochure.

An aerial view, around 1923, at the start of the development of the Cedars Estate, to the north west of Rickmansworth. The Chess Valley – which Liddell considered as a route to Chesham, Tring and the LNWR – lies to the top of the picture, with the road to Chorleywood through the trees. *(LTM)*

Grocer William Palmer was one of the enterprising shopkeepers of Rickmansworth who established a regular delivery service of essentials for the new residents of the Cedars Estate. The order was collected one day and would be delivered on the next visit, together with any local news and gossip.

The view looking west from the edge of Chorleywood Common, over the goods yard of Chorleywood station, with Darvell's coal yard. In the late 1920s, houses are beginning to spring up on both sides of the railway.

Surrounded by Metro-land, with the prospects of golf, fishing, shooting, horse riding, country walks, bracing air and a good night's sleep, the refreshed Chorleywood commuter strides off towards the station in the early morning to catch his train to work in the City.

An aerial view, looking north, over 'top' or 'new' Amersham that began to grow up around the Met station in the 1930s. The MRCE's Weller Estate is just being built around the line. The route was on the top of the hill overlooking the 'old' Amersham, because the Met could not acquire the land for the easier path. *(Colin Seabright)*

LIVE ON
THE
WELLER
ESTATE
AMERSHAM

'High and Over', designed by Amyas Connell for Professor Bernard Ashmole, was the origin of a Modernist style development at Amersham in the 1930s. Because of its distinctive 'Y' shape, it had to be camouflaged during the last war in order to prevent giving guidance to enemy bombers. *(Colin Seabright)*

The estate agents Pretty & Ellis opened at Great Missenden in 1901, soon after the arrival of the Met. They expanded after the First World War with the growth of Metro-land and this is their office adjacent to Amersham station. Mr Ellis was based here and took a personal interest in potential home buyers by meeting them on the platform. *(C Seabright)*

architect to the Met, in order to establish a style and standard for the local builders. As the MRCE estates were orientated towards the middle and upper price market, the MRCE also sold some of the larger sites to individuals for them to commission designs from a recommended list of architects. Equally, the MRCE encouraged a wide variety of speculative commercial developments complementary to their own, in order to provide a 'ladder of aspiration' – and to attract more commuters to bolster Met revenues. At one end of the scale, there were the large estates of higher-density houses and flats and, at the other extreme, spacious detached residences. Inevitably, any grander properties in the neighbourhood were highly regarded as adding 'tone' to the nearby developments. A classic example was the Moor Park estate created around the stately home of Lord Ebury, having been bought in 1920 by Lord Leverhulme's (of Lever Bros) property development company. In addition, many architect-designed individual houses of high standard were built, ranging from the 'countrified' style of the noted architect Charles Voysey (1851-1941), who built 'The Orchard' for himself in Chorleywood – often regarded as the classic exemplar of Metro-land residences – to the first 'modernist movement' building 'High and Over' in 1930, on the slopes above Old Amersham.

The Met under Watkin had acquired a large assortment of land, Selbie had continued to add to it, and then the MRCE added to the portfolio by buying adjoining and new plots. In retrospect, this stock appears to have been exploited in a rather ad hoc fashion, which makes the subsequent evolution of Metro-land estates difficult to describe in a clear chronological or geographical order. In practice, as with the problems with the long-anticipated Watford branch line, the development was influenced by the aftermath of the First World War, then there were also lengthy commercial negotiations and a host of other issues, which caused delays. However, some basic patterns do emerge:

a)   The first Watkin estate for his workers at Neasden, and the next commercial one at Willesden, were intended for those of moderate means.

b)   Further developments followed along the Extension Line towards Amersham, tending to have larger houses, but sometimes sub-divided into a range of price options.

c)   The sites along the Uxbridge branch were started later, tending to be larger developments and concentrating on the quintessential $2^{1}/_{2}$-bedroom semi-detached houses.

d)   Increasingly, speculative builders moved to develop land close to the MRCE estates in order to benefit from a synergy with the Metro-land brand.

e)   As the commuting population of Metro-land grew, the Met opened new halts and then stations to meet the demand, first closer to London, e.g. Dollis Hill and Gladstone Park (1909), and then along the Extension and the Uxbridge branch.

f) It is apparent that the MRCE had a wide range of relationships with other housing developers. The core were those more closely controlled and preferentially marketed by the MRCE, but there was a looser association with those who were only included in advertising by the company. Then there was a larger group of developers who just drew mutual benefit from developing near the MRCE. The names of these builders, such as Comben & Wakeling, Nash, Costain and Cutlers, who all erected several thousand homes, are now embedded in the collective memory of Metro-landers.

As described earlier, Watkin initiated matters in 1875 by buying several tracts of open land of about 400 acres for £175,000 in the Willesden Green/Kingsbury area for his push to Harrow and beyond. These and other surplus Met lands were exploited by the Met and MRCE as the core of their 15 Metro-land housing developments, as follows: -

Neasden Works Estate: from 1881 with 62 houses, 40 more in 1888 and 102 in 1924.
Sherrick Green Estate, between Willesden Green and Kingsbury: 41$\frac{1}{2}$ acres, 1927-30.
Willesden Park Green Estate: from 1882, extended to Walm Lane and Villiers Road in the 1890s and again in 1904, to a total of some 3,000 homes.
Kingsbury Garden Village: 40 acres, started in 1920 and including staff houses.
Chalk Hill Estate, Wembley: 123 acres started in 1921 and an added 10$\frac{1}{2}$ acres.
Wembley Park Estate Co: 280 acres bought by the railway in 1890 for sport and pleasure grounds. After demolition of Watkin's Tower in 1907, the land was sold for houses starting at Wembley Park Drive and Oakington Avenue and was extended from 1920. The eastern end was used for the 1924 British Empire Exhibition.
Woodcock Dell Estate, Northwick Park: 8$\frac{1}{2}$ acres adjoining Selfridges Sports Ground and started in 1932.
Harrow Garden Village, Rayners Lane: from 1930, 213 acres developed by E S Reid, formerly of Harrow UDC.
Eastcote Hill Estate: 10$\frac{3}{4}$ acres, from 1927.
Manor Farm & Elm Grove Estates, Ruislip: 19$\frac{1}{2}$ acres and 21$\frac{1}{2}$ acres, from 1927.
Hillingdon Mount Estate: 7$\frac{1}{2}$ acres, started in 1927.
Grange Estate, Pinner, north of line: 150 acres, started 1913 and, due to the First World War, restarted in 1920.
Cecil Park Estate, Pinner, south of line: 130 acres started in 1901-1914.
Cedars Estate, Rickmansworth, on both sides of line: 454 acres and 150 acres nearer Chorleywood with homes of various sizes, from1921 to 1932.
Weller Estate, Amersham, both sides of line: 78 acres, north to Woodside Farm and south to Batchelor's Wood. Started in 1930, with 535 houses and 51 shops.

In addition to these developments, the MRCE also sold off land that they did not require to others, such as land in Pinner and College Roads at Harrow and land at Nashleigh Hill, Chesham, from Watkin's abortive scheme to Tring.

Selbie's drive to roll out Metro-land was viewed by his GCR/LNER partners in the Joint with mixed feelings because they resented having to subscribe half of the capital to fund the consequent improvements to the Met infrastructure. Indeed, they drew the line at contributing towards inducements for potential estate developers and buyers. However, they were quite happy to take their share of the profit from the steady rise in passenger and freight traffic over the Joint.

As the Met neared its take-over by LT in 1933, the MRCE had been associated strongly with the development of about 1,500 acres of land, and unrelated developments probably representing another 1,500 acres. This is likely to have brought in the order of 20,000 extra homes to the vicinity of their line. A consequence of the MRCE success was a profit rising to some 8%, compared with the overall 3% of the Met itself. As might be expected, the size of these developments was reflected in the increase in passenger numbers and generated more profitable traffic, so that by the mid-1920s the Met was earning more than twice the amount for a third-class seat than the main line railway companies. The impact of Harrow Garden Village is a good example, for when Reid started building the number of passengers was 14,000 p.a. and some 5 years later this had risen to some 4 million p.a.! Largely as a consequence of Metro-land, from 1913 to 1937 the Met passenger revenue grew by 120%, which included dramatic increases in season tickets of five-fold and workman's tickets of fifteen-fold. There was also a commensurate rise in goods revenues from the needs of the new householders, builders and growing utility suppliers.

As might be expected, this had significant effects on population distribution. At a local level, new estates sometimes moved the 'centre of gravity' of existing towns, such as from 'old' to 'top' Amersham, or created new centres, like Little Chalfont, Rayners Lane or Northwood Hills. However, these changes were part of a much larger movement to the suburbs. Typically, Harrow showed a ten-fold growth in population from 1901 to 1930 and by 1937 numbers living in outer London had increased by 2.5 million. Contributing to this was the parallel fall of some 450,000 in the number of people living in Inner London, and the rest who came from elsewhere to commute to town or to work in local jobs with the increasing number of factories and offices locating in the Metro-land. Ironically, the decrease in population of Inner London reduced the already vulnerable Met revenues in this area, and so the boost from Metro-land was even more welcome.

ooooo0000oooooo

CHAPTER 11

LIVING IN METRO-LAND

In those halcyon days, the local Met station was the focus for those who lived in and travelled from a Metro-land estate: for the train timetable dictated the departure and arrival of the breadwinner and thus, the families mealtimes and much else. Probably most were unaware that, for those in Harrow and beyond, it would have been a 'Joint' station. This gave the option of travelling to the City (via the Met and Baker Street) or by the GCR/LNER to Marylebone, with even the possibility of using the main line to the north. The first train brought out the morning papers at about 5.30 am for breakfast delivery and, although not in the timetables, carried London night-shift workers returning from the newspapers, hospitals and markets. This train then returned with the first of the early London-bound passengers, who thereby also availed themselves of a daily Workmen's ticket. Some travelled on the early trains because they had to be at work at this time, but others because it was significantly cheaper than later fares or even season tickets. The latter also needed a substantial lump sum payment, not trivial in relation to a mortgage repayment. The peak flow began about 7.00 am and culminated with those aiming to reach the City between 9 and 10 am.

All these commuters would usually walk in converging streams towards the station, for a specific train. Nearing the station, they would probably pass a 'parade' of new shops with the essentials of food and services like a ladies' hairdressing salon, and a chemist offering 'photographic requisites' plus large glass flasks of coloured fluids glowing in its window. Well-known chains would soon also be represented by the likes of Home & Colonial, MacFisheries and International Stores. Then, almost beside the station, would be the estate agents – often in rather primitive wooden huts – usually with multiple Dickensian names such as Swannell & Sly; Stimpson, Lock & Vince; Frank, Knight & Rutley or Pretty & Ellis – where someone like Mr Ellis would be ready to greet a potential customer off the train and take them straightaway in his car (thus minimising the apparent distance) to the Metro-land estate. The stationmaster would be on duty, being a respected figure in the neighbourhood, and expected by the railway to take part in local affairs and attract business. Thus on entering the station, the regulars could expect to be acknowledged by one of the stationmen, before visiting the Wyman's newspaper and Findlay's tobacconist kiosks (both had long contracts from the Joint), or at the larger stations like Rickmansworth and Aylesbury, even a buffet. On the platform, a porter might be undertaking sweeping up any rubbish and the daily task of sprinkling Jeyes Fluid, thereby adding a distinctive aroma. Then commuters took up their customary positions on the platform, in order to be ready to join a compartment with their regular companions. Whilst waiting, the eye might wander over the familiar array of brightly-coloured enamel signs that were fixed to every available piece of wall space. Being virtually permanent, these advertised long-serving products such as:

Fry's Five Boys' Chocolate – *desperation - - realisation*   Bovril – *is liquid life!*
Lux – *won't shrink woollens*   Virol – *anaemic girls need it!*
Mazawattee Tea   Brooke Bond Dividend Tea – *and also save money!*
Cadbury's Cocoa – *absolutely pure!*   Robin Starch – *preserves your linens!*
Camp Coffee – *is the best!*   Brasso Metal Polish   Tizer – *the appetiser!*
Wincarnis - *for nerves and brain fag!*   Elliman's Embrocation
Dr W J Collis-Brownes Chlorodyne – *insurance dispensing*   Sunlight Soap
Pears' Soap – *for mother & baby too!*   Marconi – *the greatest name in wireless!*
Spratts' Bonio – *builds up a dog!*   Cherry Blossom Boot Polish – *is the best!*
Will's 'Wild Woodbine' Cigarettes   Stephens' Inks – *for all temperatures!*

These were now being superseded by the more graphic, but paper, posters carrying transitory campaigns such as: *That's Shell – That Was!* and *My Goodness, My Guinness!*

The station furniture also had an accustomed appearance, with weighing and penny-in-the-slot chocolate machines. But other items awaiting loading on the next train, such as the groups of milk churns and baskets of watercress, or possibly racing pigeons for distant release, all pleasantly confirmed that one was indeed in the country. The massive variety of parcels on the platform and on barrows for dispatch by train or local carrier to the neighbourhood added to the busy scene. This was reinforced by looking across to the goods sidings at the sight of horsebox wagons, agricultural machinery in transit, timber for furniture and loads of manure for the thin Chilterns soil. Nearby would be the coal merchants' huts of Charrington, Keen & Batchelor, Bretnall & Cleland, surrounded alike by piles of fuel in pens made from old sleepers, beside coal wagons emblazoned with the suppliers' names such as Stephenson & Clarke (Yorkshire steam coal), Phurnacite (moulded ovoids), and Ystradgynlais (anthracite), whilst the grimy coalmen weighed and filled the stiff black sacks.

The bell-code could be heard from the signal box and then the train would draw in. The Met trains had a distinctive character, with both the powerful throbbing electric locomotives and the elegant steam engines in their Victorian 'crimson-lake' liveries, hauling teak-finished Dreadnought coaches. First, one opened the heavy slam-door with its brass handle bearing the message *'Live in Metro-land'*, then stepped up onto the running-board into the all-pervasive pungent smell of steam, smoke, brake dust, leather and fusty moquette upholstery. Putting any umbrellas or bags up in the netting of the luggage rack and checking that the leather strap was holding the drop-window in the right position, one could settle onto the cushions and admire the prints and maps of Metro-land. If the train passed through 'Ricky' (Rickmansworth), one could watch possibly the fastest engine changeover in the world. Here a throbbing Bo-Bo electric locomotive – carrying an evocative nameplate like 'Sherlock Holmes' – would be swapped with one of the elegant maroon tank engines that handled the heavy trains over the Chilterns. All this with ballet-like precision within some 3 minutes to keep within the 4 allowed. Meanwhile, the station buffet served drinks at a matching rate for those passengers who made the most of the brief stop. It is of interest to reflect that the 'working' timetable of the Met was often timed to a half-minute.

Nevertheless, catching even the suburban LNER trains to Marylebone made passengers conscious that this was something different. The locomotives seemed larger, the coaches more reminiscent of a main line experience with their prints of distant places, as they sped past the busy Met stations after Harrow and arrived at a 'proper' terminus of Marylebone. Even more so, when an express from the north pulled in, hauled by an ex-GCR or a new LNER Gresley locomotive in green livery, and Metro-land travellers could take the option of partaking of tea (with sandwiches, bread, butter and preserves, plus cakes) in the restaurant car.

In the evening, the returning passengers reversed the pattern of flow, except that the service was punctuated by more main line expresses from Marylebone to the North thundering past platforms of suburban travellers at places like Moor Park & Sandy Lodge, before they retraced their steps to home. There, on the main road near the estate, would be a red Post Office telephone box, for in the early 1930s few would have an instrument in their own house – urgent messages being by a telegram delivered by a boy on a bicycle from the nearest Post Office. At the best location would be an MRCE Estate Office, selling any remaining plots (with suggestions on architects and builders) and houses (with mortgage advice), as well as a 'show' house fitted out in 'Ideal Home' style. By today's standards, one would notice few driveways or garages, a very rare television aerial, gas street lighting, pavement slabs (checked each year and relaid as necessary), and the made-up roads hand-swept by the Council would contrast with the rough, unlit 'unadopted' roads. Unseen would be the provision of the main services of gas, water, electricity, and sewerage, again in contrast with some 'unadopted' sites without utilities and often relying on the cesspits still common in the country. Lastly, one would come to the familiar front garden that would usually involve a privet hedge, well-kept lawn and roses to complete the picture. The rear garden would also centre on a lawn, but with flowerbeds, a coalbunker and the inevitable shed for multifarious activities, including resting from the efforts of dealing with the soil that the MRCE optimistically described as 'chalk, gravel and clay'. Across the back garden would be strung a washing line to dry the clothes and also a long length of copper wire as an aerial for the family wireless.

Carefully avoiding stepping on the newly Cardinal-polished front-door step, one might enter a semi-detached home via a narrow hall with stairs rising to the upstairs of 2/3 bedrooms, a small bed or 'box' room, a toilet and bathroom. Downstairs consisted of 2 rooms (living/lounge/drawing/dining) with one reserved, or preserved for visitors plus a kitchen and 'scullery'. The kitchens were often quite narrow so that it could be proudly claimed that both sides were within easy reach of the housewife. They probably contained a cooker, a range for heating water and an iron, clothes boiler, mangle and earthenware sink. All water was supplied from lead pipes and there was probably no refrigerator or central heating. The floors would be covered by a mixture of 'lino' and carpets, with parquet being the exception. And so the traveller would go to their waiting 'slippers', evening meal, favourite chair and wireless programme, Horlicks (*'worried about night starvation?'*) and thence to bed.

This represented a typical semi-detached house on a plot about 33 ft x 100 ft. However, obviously the sort of home that the traveller returned to varied significantly between Metro-land estates, but less within any one site so that they felt that 'the best was within reach'. At the upper end of the scale was the Leverhulme (of Lever Brothers, later Unilever) estate at Moor Park, with large detached houses on spacious plots surrounding the sometime house of Lord Ebury. *"Here one may enjoy the quietude and seclusion (without isolation) with all the amenities of residence in an old English Park yet without the responsibilities of its ownership. Offering facilities for sport and recreation, it affords an ideal way of entertaining and accommodating guests. Consequently the large house with spare rooms and extensive domestic staff is no longer necessary; but just a place large enough for family needs. Large gardens too can, with the necessary outdoor staff, be dispensed with."* Then, via estates like the Cedars at Rickmansworth and the Weller at Amersham, mainly with more modest detached properties and also some semi-detached houses, to the later more numerous estates of larger, denser developments with mainly semi-detached properties, such as Harrow Garden Village near Rayners Lane.

The sort of people who lived in pre-war Metro-land were inevitably as varied as the different types of estate, but, as with the houses, the spread within a particular one was quite narrow. From my personal experience of a semi-detached home on a Metro-land estate near Harrow, initially the majority of husbands were white-collar staff working in the Civil Service, education, local government, or banks, large companies and similar organisations, providing what most people regarded as permanent employment. At this time around 1930, many of these men had served in the First World War and felt lucky to be alive. The typical working week was of about 48 hours, which included Saturday mornings (although office

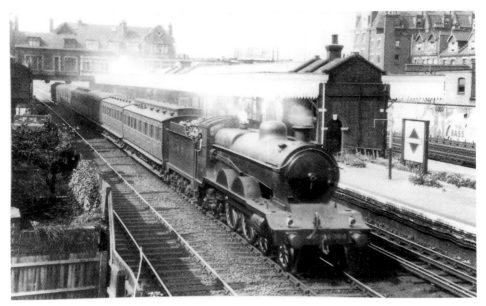

In 1923 the plethora of railway companies in the UK were merged into the 'big four' – except the Met! The GCR became part of the LNER, but little changed at first, as here at West Hampstead where an ex-GCR C4 no.6086, with a motley array of coaches behind, heads for Marylebone. The Met diamond logo is still there on the platform. *(Real Photos)*

But by the mid-1930s, the LNER presence was apparent. This traditional 3.20 pm down 'Sheffield Special' has just passed Rickmansworth, and is still headed by an ex-GCR 4-4-0 Director no.5437 'Prince George'. However, the second engine is a new Gresley B17 4-6-0 and foreshadows the increasing influence of the LNER. *(Ian Jeayes)*

Apart from introducing his own new designs, the LNER's CME, Sir Nigel Gresley, modified some of the GCR engines. One of these, no.6168, is being prepared under the eye of the foreman for a special train at Neasden shed, 1932. The ex-GCR 4-6-0 had been fitted with Caprotti valve gear and showed reduced coal consumption. (*Getty Images*)

A 1931 Marylebone-bound excursion train near Willesden Green Met. It is headed by an ex-GCR Robinson Class 8B 4-4-2 express passenger locomotive. It formed one of Gresley's experiments comparing relative merits of 4-4-2 and 4-6-0 wheel arrangements. Now in LNER livery and a class C4, it was based at Neasden for most of its life. (*NRM*)

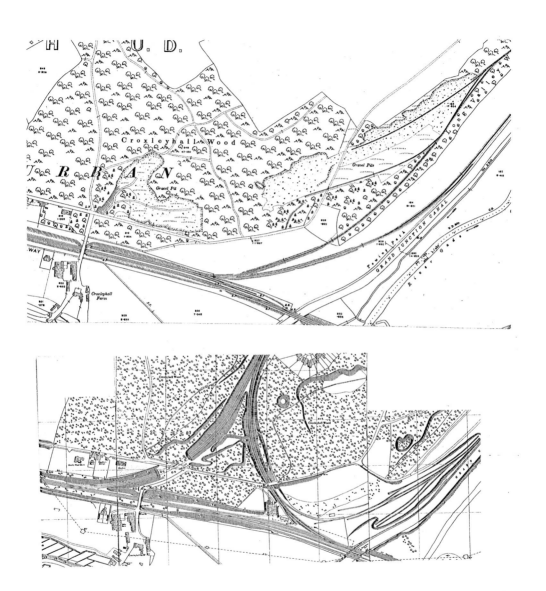

Maps showing layout of the Met where it crosses the River Gade and the Grand Union Canal, near Rickmansworth. Top: The gravel pits of Lord Ebury provided an excellent source of gravel and were connected by sidings in the 1890s. Below: Later, the 1925 branch to Watford used this land and retained some sidings as a tip for Met spoil.

Construction of the Watford branch was delayed by the First World War and then by problems with the water-logged ground. Here, an over-bridge is being built near the only intermediate station, at Croxley Green. By this time the Met's partner in the Joint was the LNER, and so this branch came under the auspices of the Met & LNER Joint Committee.

A 1930s view, looking north, of the triangular Watford South Junction with the branch and the Met main line. The signal box is in front of the Met electric substation, whilst a Baker Street-bound train of T stock approaches. The signalman had little to do, as the service from Rickmansworth to Watford was soon dropped due to lack of use. *(LTM)*

One of the reasons for the unpopularity of the Rickmansworth-Watford service was the location of the Met station, far from the centre of Watford. To counter this, Selbie bought some land in the High St for another station, and this map from his papers shows the ideas for a tunnel to extend the branch to this more advantageous site. *(C Foxell/ LMA)*

Top: The arrival of the inaugural train and VIPs at Watford on 31st October 1925.
Mid: Empress Tea Rooms in Watford High St, acquired by the Met for a new station.
Bott: The Met established a bus service to take passengers from the station to the town.

With the opening of the Watford branch in 1925, electrification was extended to Rickmansworth. This became where the traction had to be changed to steam haulage for the route over the Chilterns and then back again on the return run. It was a slick operation, scheduled at less than 3 minutes, of which the Met was proud. All the participants knew their roles, although their actions would probably not be permitted by current safety regulations. The top picture shows, in BR days, an ER LI 2-6-4T being uncoupled, whilst below, a Met Bo-Bo is backing on for the journey to Baker St. *(LTM)*

Selbie had long wanted an appropriate headquarters for the Met at Baker Street, but the First World War delayed matters and it was not finished until 1929. Chiltern Court was also built over the station with prestigious flats, & restaurant etc, as shown above. *(LTM)*

The last defiant gesture of the Met, before being absorbed by London Transport, was the construction of their branch from Wembley Park to Stanmore. Begun in 1930, heavy rain delayed matters, as usual in this area. This shows the contractor's Manning Wardle 0-6-0 saddle tank engine working on a temporary track near the Wealdstone Brook. *(CAF Coll)*

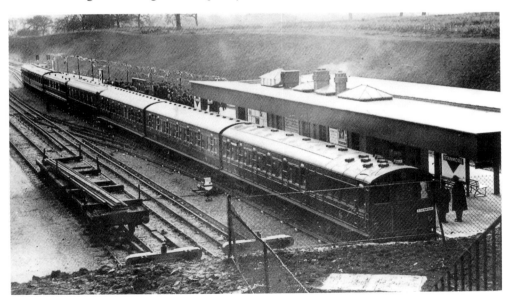

The formal opening of the Stanmore line on 9th December 1932, with a crowd on the bunting-bedecked platform welcoming the VIPs. Extensive goods facilities, including those for horses and cattle were provided, more in hope than justification, for soon the surrounding countryside would become the latest addition to Metro-land. *(LTM)*

The VIPs arrived at Stanmore in a Pullman and the penultimate outing of the Met Director's venerable coach. Walking towards the station are (left-right): Sir Cunliffe-Lister MP; Lord Aberconway, Chairman of the Met; P J Pybus MP, Minister for Transport (who encouraged the creation of LT); and Mr John Anderson, Met GM. *(LTM)*

For the off-peak service on the Stanmore line, some T stock electric cars were employed. These had earlier been converted for single-car operation to provide a shuttle facility for the short-lived Rickmansworth–Watford service in 1925. Here, one glides towards Wembley Park in solitary splendour during the late 1930s. *(Clive Foxell Collection)*

workers were allowed to wear more casual clothes on this day!). A few single women with secure jobs such as a telephone operator supervisor, or of independent means, had houses, often supporting older relations. However, although not many wives proclaimed working, daughters might have jobs in London or locally, as the infrastructure grew with the influx of new homeowners. This local development made service trades more affluent and the owners and managers began to move into the estates. This service economy is illustrated by the variety of tradesmen that called at our home: the milkman twice a day, with a horse-drawn cart; the baker once a day, with a large upright barrow on two wheels, the handles of which lifted him off the ground when going down hill; the postman thrice; the butcher's boy by bicycle twice a week; and the grocer twice a week. Others, like the coalman or the Gas, Light & Coke Co. in their steam-powered Sentinel lorry, also made regular deliveries. Over a longer period, visits could be expected from the men from the Prudential, Hoover, Singer and the like – all using a service call to take the opportunity to sell new products. There was something reassuring about seeing such familiar faces and catching up with the latest gossip. In addition, there were the itinerant callers such as the Walls Ice Cream man on his tricycle as well as the French onion sellers, gypsies with pegs and posies, rag and bone men, tinkers and the knife-sharpeners with their pedal-driven grinding wheels.

Painters, decorators, plumbers and electricians grew in number, in those days before DIY became popular, as subtle improvements in what were basically the same houses were significant in a hierarchy increasingly driven by 'keeping up with the Jones's'. This race was also given impetus by the acquisition of the latest 'labour saving' appliances funded by hire purchase arrangements.

As Metro-land became a victim of its own success, the pressure on land grew with a consequent increase in prices, and this led to the construction of a greater proportion of higher density housing. Inevitably, potential homeowners became more willing to consider travelling further from London for the benefit of a more rural environment. As the land closer to London became fully developed, particularly to Harrow and along the Uxbridge branch, so the original concepts of rural tranquillity could only be applied to the outer reaches of the Met Line.

Although nostalgia is never what it used to be, we do tend to look back on the Metro-land of the 1920s and 1930s as a golden era. But of course in retrospect, whilst some aspects were simpler and quite pleasant, the overall quality of life reflected a labour-intensive, shorter existence of greater hardship for many. Unemployment remained a possibility and, with poignant memories of the First World War still fresh in people's memories, the clouds of war were worryingly gathering yet again in the 1930s. Nevertheless, it was a time of widening horizons with the growing adult popularity of the wireless, Penguin and Gollancz books, and magazines like *Picture Post*. As well as a range of outdoor pursuits such as cycling, hiking and tennis, there was also the healthy annual holiday to plan with help from the latest LNER *Holiday Handbook* (3d) obtained from the station. For the children there were the attractions of Scouts and Guides, the likes of Hornby and the *Meccano Magazine*, the latest *Just William* or *Enid Blyton* book, plus the weekly comic. The nearest town held the escapist attractions of Shipman & King's cinemas and emporia like Woolworths (everything less than 6d) and Marks & Spencers (less than 5/-).

The perception of Metro-land has also been coloured by depreciating comments about the negative connotations of such a seamless suburbia, ironically even by those who lived there. For example, often those living on one of the innocuous estates in Rayners Lane, South Harrow, West Harrow, North Harrow, Wealdstone or Kenton would say that they came from the rather grander sounding 'Harrow'. This attitude probably started as a defensive response to the Victorian opinion that the new suburbs broke down the clear distinction between the separate joys of the sophisticated town and the bucolic country. Of course this was at a time when the countryside around London began at Finchley Road. Even the social reformers, who had originally welcomed the idea of the provision of improved housing well outside the towns in which most worked, began to query it for the pragmatic reason that the consequent excessive time taken travelling to and from work was weakening family life – the very thing that suburban living was supposed to improve. To some extent this was true, but it ignored the real advantages of such a better environment, for most residents felt that Metro-land homes showed a considerable improvement on what had gone before. And the alternative of everyone living adjacent to his or her work was now blatantly impractical.

However, in spite of the ongoing criticism of the 'sameness' of the estates of Metro-land – implying a repetitive style giving a loss of identity – many occupants actually welcomed the reassurance of order and uniformity. Also in typical British fashion, individuality was soon seen in relatively small variations in decorative embellishments which had a cumulative effect as houses changed ownership. In addition, the passage of time transformed the aspect of many of the houses and, with growth of foliage, it matured and mellowed the overall appearance. Indeed, as the density of recent suburban housing has increased, with smaller gardens and a greater proportion of flats and town houses, so the pre-war Metro-land properties have become relatively more desirable. Indeed, the current high regard – and price – of such homes shows the gradual change in attitude, bringing Metro-land houses back into favour.

ooooo0000000ooooo

CHAPTER 12

SWAN SONG

In some ways the very success of the Metro-land campaign was to create problems for the Met in meeting the resulting growth in commuting. This came to a head with the electrification to Rickmansworth and the opening of the branch to Watford, after being delayed until 1925 due to the First World War. With the continued increase in passengers from the existing housing developments along the line, and particularly the Uxbridge branch, four troublesome congestion points had arisen that were limiting any increase in the number of trains. The first came from the conflicting movement of Extension and Uxbridge trains at the junction just north of Harrow. The delay in solving this arose from the reluctance of the London & North Eastern Railway (LNER) to fund their Joint share of replacing the points by a fly-under. However, eventually Selbie negotiated a compromise and the improvement work was completed in time to cope with the extra trains generated by the new Watford branch.

The second limiting factor was the remaining length of the only two Met tracks (the other two to Marylebone being leased to the LNER under the Joint Agreement) between Wembley Park and Harrow. The upgrade to separate slow and fast lines was finally completed in 1932. However, a third bottleneck was also growing at Finchley Road station, where the trains were concentrated into the original underground double tracks into Baker Street and the Circle Line. This problem increased in severity as the upgrades to four-tracking advanced north to Wembley Park in 1914 and thence to Harrow. From 1921, Selbie vigorously tried to solve this restriction with a number of attempts to bypass the original tunnel and Baker Street station with a new tunnel, as follows:

a) 1921: Finchley Road to King' Cross.
b) 1924: Finchley Road to King's Cross via Primrose Hill.
c) 1924: West Hampstead to Liverpool Street.
e) 1925: Kilburn to Edgware Road.
f) 1930: West Hampstead to Baker Street.
g) 1931: West Hampstead to Great Portland Street.

Some of these failed due to lack of Government support on safety grounds, for now any new tunnels were not permitted to be used by slam-door stock. Other solutions were rejected by Selbie's Board on the grounds of cost: so it remained an outstanding challenge for the successors to the Met.

The last basic obstacle to the flow of traffic remained that caused by the interlacing of the incompatible suburban Met and faster main line GCR (and now LNER) trains, which was now getting worse as the Met ran more services. Both sides recognised the causes, but the Met had insufficient leverage to influence the LNER timekeeping or to get them to collaborate on a more radical solution.

The branch to Watford turned out to be a mixed blessing, for whilst Metro-land development grew rapidly around the intermediate station at Croxley Green, the location of the Met station at Watford itself had been relegated by the Council to the periphery of the town. Several attempts by Selbie to extend the line to a more central site adjacent to the High Street, were to no avail, but housing estates did eventually grow up around the existing station.

In many ways it was appropriate that, as a final act of independence just before they were absorbed into LT, the Met built their new branch to Stanmore for the last phase of their campaign to extend Metro-land to the north. On 9th December 1932, the new line was formally opened by a special train for the VIPs and Press, headed by a pristine rake of multiple-electric T stock, a Met Pullman and, suitably, a penultimate splendid outing for their own Directors' saloon. This had been created at Neasden Works, from Lord Rothschild's original two smaller private saloons of 1895, by mounting them on a single chassis. Such was the character of the Met.

ooooo0000ooooo

CHAPTER 13

OTHERS TAKE THE REINS

After Selbie's untimely death in 1930, the absorption of the Met by LT became a just a question of the Chairman, Lord Aberconway, obtaining the best terms, until after a proud and eventful life of 69 years, it was finally subsumed into LT on 30th June 1933.

London Transport had its origins in the world's first deep-level underground 'tube' railway, the City & South London, which opened in 1890, and was quickly followed by the embryonic 'Northern' and 'Central' lines. All lost money, but attracted American investors, which led to a series of their entrepreneurs becoming actively involved in the management and evolution of the London tubes. Whittaker Wright created the Bakerloo, but after his suicide, Charles Tyson Yerkes, who had strong views on electrification using the 600v dc 4-rail system, was able to group together a number of the tube lines and also the MDR. He added the 'Piccadilly' tube to the portfolio just before he died in 1906. Soon afterwards, another American, albeit of English extraction, Albert Stanley (formerly Knattriess), became MD of the Underground Electric Railways group. After a spell in the Government, he returned in 1933 as Lord Ashfield, to lead the new over-arching London Passenger Transport Board in a relentless manner. However, it was his MD, Frank Pick, who came from the NER and thence the Underground Group, who brought detailed management and co-ordination across the breadth of LT's buses, trams and trains. A moderniser, he sought to create a harmonised and efficient system to encourage the London public to travel. It was his personal interest to employ design and art to make travel on LT a more amenable, and possibly uplifting experience, widening travellers' horizons to the attractions and opportunities of London, its city events and countryside. The latter included the former Metro-land, but not in name! Pick harnessed the abilities of leading artists, architects (Charles Holden), designers and, with his characteristic attention to detail, even Gertrude Jekyll's brother as a garden advisor. He was loath to delegate and monitored the details of implementing his plans, to the extent that others said 'decision came easily to him'. But although this made him seem prickly with colleagues, he was able to motivate and harness their talents to implement a coherent and consistent transport system for London out of many disparate elements. They were bound together by his sense of social responsibility and the visible introduction of a modern, uplifting and fit-for-purpose style, covering everything from typefaces and posters, to trains and stations. As a result, LT became instantly recognisable by an uncluttered and harmonious style. On the outbreak of the last War, Pick became Director-General of Information, but was sacked by Churchill after a disagreement on a matter of principle and died shortly afterwards.

One can well imagine the reactions of both sides when Pick and the Met came together in 1933. The Met had an impressive and unbroken history of some 69 years and regarded itself as a main line, whereas Pick came from a massive ongoing battle to unify London's diverse transport. As usual, Pick personally examined the Met in great detail and this is one of his typical memos:

"Coming down the Met from Moor Park to Baker Street and leaving Moor Park at 10.15 and arriving at Baker Street at say 11.15, stopping at Harrow and Finchley Road stations, I was surprised to find how many of the people employed upon work on the line were, so to speak, idle. For instance at Harrow station I should say that fully one-third of the men were gossiping rather than working. At two or three points on the line I noticed signal-fitting staff doing no work at all. At Northwick Park no one could say that the work was being pushed with any vigour. At Finchley Road there was a slackness pervading the whole appearance of the work. It therefore occurred to me that something was wrong with the supervision of work on the Met. Will you please tell me who is in charge and to what extent there is regular supervision of the work down this line."

There were many more like this, and one can understand his incredulous reactions to their old 'Spanish' customs', such as the Met railwayman who often used to travel to work on a convenient 'non-stop' train that always seemed to halt where he worked at Wembley Park, because the communication cord pulled itself!

Many of the Met staff had been in competition with the Underground for years and had seen Selbie manoeuvring to avoid the inevitable acquisition by LT. They regarded the subsequent actions of Pick as confirming their suspicions that he would take revenge on the independently-minded Met after the long struggle for control. Equally, those interested in railway history have often regarded Pick as destroying the essence of the Met, with the steady elimination of much of its variety and charm. So, resentment came more from the imposition of Pick's LT management, organisation and style than from the consequences of his long overdue tackling of the major operational problems of the Met. Indeed, whilst his behaviour towards the Met could be critical, as in comments like 'the Met only went to Aylesbury by accident', a dispassionate consideration of his actions tends to lead to a more favourable view, as being motivated mainly by taking a strategic approach to improving the Met system.

The Metro-land estate developers along the Stanmore line soon wanted another intermediate station on the branch. So one was built called Queensbury, to counterpoint the existing Kingsbury, but now in 1933 it was started by the new owners, London Transport, with their UndergrounD logo. *(LTM)*

London Transport immediately dropped the Metro-land brand and replaced it with a more general campaign, not linked to specific developers. Nevertheless, Frank Pick, the LT Managing Director, saw the financial advantages of the Met collaboration with its estates arm, but he failed to convince the Government that it was right for LT to act as a property developer.

Pick performed a thorough review of the individualistic Met operations and practices, seeking harmonisation with LT. This LT inspection train, with the Rothschild saloon and a Pullman behind Met no.110, is passing Chorleywood on 23rd July 1935 to examine, and then recommend, closure of the Brill branch. It shut on 30th November 1935. *(LTM)*

The last days of the quaint Wotton Tramway, O&AT and Brill branch of the Met before closure. It was offered back to Earl Temple, descendant of the Duke of Buckingham who built it for his estate. The train at Quainton Road and bound for Brill, is a pensioned-off Met class A tank engine no.41, with rigid 8-wheeler coach and few passengers. *(H.C.C.)*

Pick saw the Met steam engines as anomalous to an electrified LT and got the LNER to take responsibility for hauling these services. Equally, he made plans for electrifying the Met to Amersham and Chesham, but as an interim measure tried the use of the GWR's new diesel railcars. Here is their AEC-built no.16 on test at Chesham in 1936. *(Ray East)*

This picture shows that there have always been problems with high-density suburban rail services. In April 1934, passengers are walking along the LNER tracks to West Hampstead station after their LT train was halted due to a crash further along the line. It also shows how attitudes to safety have changed! *(Getty Images)*

In 1937, most LT locos were transferred to the LNER and sent for overhauls by their new owners. To fill the gaps, LNER A5, N5 and other types were used over the Joint. Here is an ex-GCR C14 4-4-2T hauling a rake of Met coaches. Although the C13s became common, this longer-range version was something of a rarity on this line.*(Robert Barker)*

Aylesbury station, looking northwards. On the extreme left is the engine shed shared between the GWR, LNER & Met that ran the station through their joint companies. Next the platform mainly used by the GWR, then the main lines to the north and on the right a LNER A5 4-6-2T, on a Met train to the change-over at Rickmansworth.*(Henry Priestley)*

By the late 1930s the impact on the Joint of the earlier changes of ownership were beginning to be seen and the Bo-Bo electric loco now carries the London Transport sign. But the Met Diamond logo is still on display at Baker Street station, whilst the crew of no.19 'John Wycliffe' take a break on the platform before departure. *(Len's of Sutton)*

By 1937, the ex-GCR Robinson engines that had handled the Marylebone expresses were beginning to be replaced by the new LNER Gresley types. Seen just after leaving Rickmansworth station for Woodford, is No.2853 'Huddersfield Town', one of the later 'footballers' of the B17 class of 4-6-0 locomotives. *(John Parnham)*

Under the Joint arrangements during the1930s, the LNER provided the push-pull service between Aylesbury and Verney Junction. The usual locomotive was an ex-GER engine class F7 2-4-2 T no.8307, which was fitted for auto-train working. Here is a rare picture of it, south of Northwood, on its way from Aylesbury to Neasden Shed. *(John Parnham)*

With all freight duties now being undertaken by the LNER and most ex-Met engines shedded at Neasden, the LT retained a few Met locos for maintenance duties. During the late 1930s, ex-Met F class 0-6-2T no.93, now in LT livery and numbered L52, is on such an empty train from Croxley Tip, passing Northwood Yard on the right. *(John Parnham)*

Undoubtedly Pick's analysis of the Met's major operational problems really only confirmed what Selbie had already realised, namely the desirability of complete electrification, and the easing of the Met/LNER congestion north of Harrow and the bottleneck between Finchley Road and Baker Street. But, whereas Selbie lacked the resources to attack these issues, Ashfield and Pick had both the means and the 'clout' to actually do something, and so planning commenced on practical solutions.

Thus negotiations started with Sir Ralph Wedgwood of the LNER with the objective of streamlining all the collaborative activities with LT. In the case of the Met, eliminating their 'anomalous' steam traction was seen as an essential preparatory step towards electrification, which resulted in the transfer of most Met engines to the LNER in 1937 to haul most of the remaining Met steam trains. This made an unfortunate impression on the Met crews involved, and the other inevitable decision to integrate some Met facilities into the larger LT organisation, such as Neasden becoming subservient to Acton Works, were taken in a manner which alienated the Met staff. With time, the distinctive personality of the Met seemed to fade with the teak becoming brown, without lining, and the remaining steam engines first being lettered 'MET'– rather than the grander 'Metropolitan'. Then 'London Transport', to be replaced by plain black LNER engines. But one notable exception to this trend was the surprising retention by LT of the Met Pullman cars that plied between the City and the farthest reaches of Metro-land, carrying passengers for an extra shilling in a style to which they wished to become accustomed. It is certainly odd that such an anomalous service continued under Pick, but it now appears that Lord Ashfield and the subsequent Chairman of LT, Sir John Elliott, were both directors of the Pullman Co. and also used their staff to train the chefs at the LT headquarters in 55 Broadway!

Pick's detailed analysis of the services over the Joint line showed that the incompatibility of the Met and LNER services was even worse than feared, with the poor time-keeping of the daily 23 fast LNER trains causing almost 6 times as much delay to the Met services. Thus by 1935, plans were agreed with the LNER and well advanced for the addition of two extra tracks to Rickmansworth for fast Met and the LNER trains, plus electrification of the Extension to Amersham and Chesham. However, as an interim measure, in 1936, LT borrowed one of the GWR's new streamlined AEC diesel railcars for trials on the Chesham branch to replace the steam 'Shuttle'. It was found to have insufficient capacity and work was started on a more powerful version at Acton Works, but halted with the outbreak of war. War also stopped the preparatory civil engineering on the modernisation beyond Harrow and the complementary Acton development of the new multiple-electric stock. The other matter resolved with the LNER was the reduction of services over the old A&BR, including closure of the venerable Brill branch in 1935.

The proactive Met promotion of Metro-land by extolling specific MRCE estates ceased with their separation from the MRCE following the absorption by LT in 1933, but for a while, LT did display a few posters on the specific merits of living in the area and issued lists of relevant estate agents. Instead, they gave emphasis to a broad campaign extolling the attractions of accessing the local countryside by LT's trains and buses. Also LT continued to enhance the Stanmore line with a new station at Queensbury to support the inevitable estate developments, rebuilt Rayners Lane, Eastcote and Uxbridge, and created a completely new station at Northwood Hills – all in the Holden-LT style. The last such project before the war was the sweeping redevelopment of Harrow-on-the-Hill station, begun in 1938.

The MRCE had soon become a completely independent company, without any special relationship with LT. It continued to exploit its existing originally Met estates, but in any case the effects of the 1930s depression was causing the housing market to decline and they increasingly turned to more general property development. After the last war they were absorbed into a larger group.

But perhaps contrary to common belief, Pick had become somewhat envious of the way in which the Met had profitably developed Metro-land. He found that one estate developer, George Cross, had acquired some 70 acres of land near Stanmore for £12,500 in 1919 and, by constructing houses on it had generated a profit of some £56,000 by 1925. In general terms, he observed that as soon as such a railway was mooted, the land value was doubled, and when the line was actually built, the land quadrupled in value. Against this background, Pick was keen to support developments of the 'Metro-land' type and, more importantly, extend the principle to the other major new extensions that he envisaged of the LT system, in order to finance the growing LT investment programme. Therefore, in 1938 he proposed to the Barlow Commission that such exploitation of railway land should be allowed by LT as a method for financing the improvement of public transport in London. But MPs remained of the view that railways should not now benefit from an improvement in land values that they had contrived. However, LT was fortunate in receiving considerable public funding to support its' major 'New Works' modernisation plans as part of Government relief for the pre-war unemployment problems.

With the gathering threat of war and the depletion of surplus land, the expansion of Metro-land began to slow, and with it Met revenues. At the same time, there were the first signs of a reaction against the spread of the LT system ever further into the countryside, with the consequent damage that housing estates brought. The turning point came in 1937, when work started on a new LT extension from Edgware to Bushey Heath, with a major depot at Aldenham, leading to protests over inappropriate urbanisation which delayed matters, so that work did not restart until after the War.

Surprisingly, there was little public resistance to Pick's imposition of a pervasive modern LT culture – except from Metro-land, where some Pinner residents launched a petition against their primitive wooden station being replaced by a modern Holden-designed LT station, similar to nearby Harrow. They wanted a 'medieval look' in keeping with the surroundings, and so much of the original wooden structure remains until this day!

The last significant LT improvement to be completed just before the outbreak of war in 1939 was relief for the other long-standing bottleneck, at Finchley Road. This was achieved by rearranging the existing four tracks between Harrow and Finchley Road, with the slow stopping trains running between the outer fast tracks. In addition, LT had been able to extend their Bakerloo tube north from Baker Street to Finchley Road, by tunnels under the Met, and thence to run over slow tracks to Stanmore. This took over the Met's stopping services to Wembley Park and Stanmore, to at last produce a substantial easement of the congestion into Baker Street.

The War brought an end to all LT's New Works Programme, and so the civil engineering works beyond Harrow were 'mothballed' for the duration. Some modifications were made to ease wartime operations, such as a new junction at Shepherds Furze near Calvert between the old GCR and LNWR lines, to take the heavy rail traffic avoiding London. Operational changes were also made, such as on the Chesham branch, where a push-pull shuttle was introduced using ex-GCR C13 tank engines with veteran Met Ashbury coaches. But in general, it was a case of using existing equipment with minimal maintenance and undertaking rapid repairs to the damage caused by the extensive bombing and the later V-weapon attacks.

ooooo0000ooooo

CHAPTER 14

POST-WAR UPS AND DOWNS

The outbreak of the last war in 1939 marked the suspension of the expansion of Metro-land. But as indicated in the last chapter, it was already apparent by that time that reservations were mounting about the form of higher density development increasingly associated with it, and the way in which this was engulfing the countryside. The War itself inevitably overloaded and denuded civil resources, and affected the state of our infrastructure and the ability to repair it, let alone improve it. Whilst many plans were made for post-war development, like that by Abercrombie for London, little happened in practice. This bleak situation persisted, with some form of food rationing continuing until the 1950s, and Britain's overall financial predicament restricted capital investment for everything from housing to railways. To some extent, the turmoil caused by the wholesale nationalisation of most of the country's 'utility' companies masked their run-down condition. Whilst the new Labour Government's unification of a host of separate companies into British Transport Commission, the National Coal Board, British Gas etc., produced some improvements through rationalisation and economies of scale, the investment was still not available to even catch-up with the lack of wartime maintenance.

In a strange way, one of the effects of the War and its difficult economic aftermath was to prolong the old-fashioned ambience of the Met & GC Joint line. Firstly the older employees, with their memories of the Joint and its ways, had been encouraged to stay, and even the retired had been asked to return to work to help during the shortage of staff. Secondly, with the emphasis on armaments, there was a lack of new equipment, so some redundant Ashbury electric stock dating from 1898 had been converted back to steam operation for the Chesham branch, thus releasing their 'Dreadnoughts' for main line use. It also prolonged the use of all the original Met stock well after the end of the War, so that an ex-Met tank engine could often be seen at Rickmansworth and elsewhere, helping out when the LNER or BR had no locomotives available. Shortages also meant that the main line was still graced by some of Robinson's finest creations for the GCR, from grimy, but magnificent, Directors, to humble C13 tank engines.

Confidence was slow to return, but the 1951 Festival of Britain provided a focus for hopes of a better quality of living, and gradually resources became available. With the railways, the British Transport Commission launched a massive 'modernisation programme' in 1955 to eliminate steam, introduce diesel or electric traction, and renew the track and signalling. Housing was another priority, with high-rise tower blocks and the building of major 'new towns' at Milton Keynes, Stevenage and elsewhere, as well as large estates on the periphery of London for its over-spill. However, in these instances, as well as in most other areas, it is difficult to claim that in the urge to make improvements, the investments were wisely made. With the benefit of hindsight, it is easy to see where such ambitious programmes went wrong: with the rush to abolish steam locomotives, a multiplicity of types of diesels were launched, many of which were unsatisfactory. Equally, for housing, the disadvantages of the rapid expansion of the utilitarian tower blocks, large estates and new towns are now only too apparent.

These major building schemes only partly met the post-war pent-up demand for affordable housing. And after the War, in the old Metro-land, a lot of development leapt over the Green Belt on the north-west of London to encompass towns such as High Wycombe, Aylesbury and Hemel Hempstead.

The new BR only exploited their surplus land for major commercial office and retail developments and as the old MRCE ceased its housing activities, the continuing repressed demand for affordable homes in Metro-land was met largely by council estates and speculative builders. The latter squeezed houses into the few gaps remaining close to London, demolished detached properties with large gardens for redevelopment with groups of smaller homes and, further out, created larger new estates. As with the high-rise flats and similar buildings, some employing new unit-construction techniques later developed structural problems.

Inevitably, such post-war housing developments with their associated motorway and trunk roads have left Metro-land somewhat isolated and marooned in a 1930s time-warp which leaves the residents in something of a dilemma. On one hand, they desire improvements in infrastructure with better employment, roads, parking, supermarkets and hospitals – but the 'Not In My Back Yard' aspect is a powerful deterrent. Such conflicts inevitably involve the ongoing deterioration of the Green Belt.

The effect of the 1948 nationalisation on the railways of Metro-land was dramatic: the LT and LNER partners in the Joint were both part of BTC, with nominally uniform practices and rules. However, BR inevitably had to divide its empire up into manageable segments and then allocate them routes to operate. Whilst the old Joint arrangements continued to be used to oversee the familiar lines through Metro-land, the partners changed with the varying whims of government and the upper echelons of BR. During this, the LPTB went through a number of metamorphoses,

All parts of the Met, LNER and Joint lines were damaged by bombing during the first part of the last War. Here, one of the bombs that fell on Baker Street station during May 1941 hit offices over the station and the clear-up continues with a T stock multiple- electric unit standing below in platform no.3. *(LTM)*

In the last part of the War, conventional bombing raids by German aircraft were replaced by strikes from pilot-less weapons. In 1944, the V1 flying bombs were launched from across the Channel, and here is the scene where one nearly struck a Met line Q stock train near Wembley Park. Later there was much damage from the V2 rocket attacks.

Part of the pre-war LT New Works Programme for improving the Met Extension included a new fleet of multiple-electric stock. A number of mock-ups were prepared to try various seating configurations. After the War two Met T stock chassis were used to test the best options. This is an artist's drawing of experimental car No.17000. *(LTM)*

For safety reasons in tunnels, sliding doors were now essential on new stock and interiors had to be a compromise between the short high-density town use and the longer distance Metro-land requirements, with more comfortable seats and luggage racks. Above, experimental car No.17000 was completed and trialed in 1946, but not adopted. *(LTM)*

One of the first pre-war projects to be completed on the Joint was the long-overdue completion of the four-tracking of the Met line at Harrow, which involved a simplification of the layout for the Uxbridge fly-under Junction. *(LTM)*

1948 also saw the nationalisation of the railways, including LT, under the BTC, and this picture of an ex-LNER class N5 0-6-2T shows the first type of British Railways logo. The train is the rarely photographed coal delivery for the Gas, Light & Coke Co. works at South Harrow, leaving Rayners Lane before reversal into the retort siding. *(J Parnham)*

The LNER Thompson-designed class L1 2-6-4 tank engines were introduced from 1945 and building continued into BR days. A number were allocated to Neasden for the Marylebone suburban services and here, around 1951, is no.67758, also with a 'British Railways' logo, on an up local train of ex-Met Dreadnoughts near Wendover. *(NRM)*

During 1955, renewal of the bridge over the Regent's Canal led to Met services being diverted into Marylebone. Here, such a train of Dreadnought coaches with two ER L1 2-6-4 tank engines is heading south from near Rickmansworth. Presumably, the opportunity is being taken to transfer the rear engine to Neasden Depot. *(Les Reason)*

The post-war Marylebone expresses were intended to replace the 'Sheffield Special' of the old GCR days. Here is the 10.00 am 'The South Yorkshireman' from Bradford, about to pass Moor Park station in 1948. In new British Railways livery, it is headed by no.1299, a LNER class B1 4-6-0, built by Thompson during the War. (*Ken Nunn/LCGB*)

Later in August 1957, towards the end of the reign of the Marylebone express services, the up 'Master Cutler' coasts through Aylesbury station admired by the passengers waiting for other trains. One of the regular engines on this turn, ex-LNER Gresley class A3 4-6-2 no.60102 'Sir Frederick Banbury', hauls the train. (*Dr G C Farnell/BCRO*)

Under the stewardship of the Eastern Region of BR in the 1950s, the Marylebone services retained some former glory, with six trains per day to destinations such as Sheffield and Manchester. When 'The South Yorkshireman' paused at Rickmansworth in May 1956, *Les Reason* was able to capture this picture of the crew of A3 no.60107 'Royal Lancer'.

The other end of the ER locomotive range saw an ex-GCR Robinson 0-6-0 of 1901, now BR class J11 no.64327, with a pick-up goods. It is emerging from Croxley Tunnel, running tender-first on the south curve from Watford. In 1958, the Midland Region (BR) took over and regarded the Marylebone services as competing their own. *(Les Reason)*

In 1962, Midland Region began a major redevelopment of Euston and thus was reluctantly forced to use Marylebone as the London terminus for some of its services. Here at Rickmansworth, an up excursion is hauled by a BR Britannia class 4-6-2 no.70048 'The Territorial Army 1908-1958', then based at Neasden. (*Stephen Gradidge*)

The footbridge over the Met just at the southern end of Rickmansworth station was a favourite spot for watching the busy scene. Met-Vick Bo-Bo no.5 'John Hampden' appropriately heads an Aylesbury train of Dreadnought coaches, whilst in the siding the BR tank loco, which has brought in an up train, waits to run back. (*Stephen Gradidge*)

The old Met F class 0-6-2T tank engines were withdrawn from 1957, being beyond economic overhaul. In their last years they were often seen with LT's Ransome & Rapier crane and breakdown train. L50 (ex-Met no.91) is passing the little-used north curve of Watford South Junction, en-route to Amersham, early in 1958. *(S Gradidge)*

LT began to replace its ageing fleet of Met steam engines in 1956. These had been retained in 1937 for engineering and back-up duties, when most had been transferred to the LNER. One of the daily runs was to Croxley waste tip at Watford South Junction and here, new L91 (ex-GW no.5752) waits in sight of the sub-station. *(Les Reason)*

via London Transport Executive and London Underground Ltd, and the Met's character became steadily subsumed into its parent. However, in practice, it was the more constant partner in the Joint during the BR regime. Indeed as economic conditions improved after the War, they were able to revive a version of their pre-war New Works Programme for rejuvenating the Met Extension. This involved adding extra fast tracks for the Marylebone trains to ease the bottlenecks beyond Harrow to Rickmansworth, and extending their electrification to Chesham and Amersham, where now BR took over. This major improvement was completed in 1961, being operated by a fleet of new A60 aluminium multiple-electric units, which continue to the present day.

By contrast, the old GCR/LNER line was geographically separate from the rest of its main network, the Eastern Region. Moreover, it was now sandwiched between the Western Region (GWR) and Midland Region (LMR), so all three had claims to take it over. Initially, it fell to the Eastern Region and, with shortages of locomotives and greater freedom of exchange within their territory, the pattern of engines on the Joint swung from the classic GCR types (such as Robinson's Directors) to the LNER replacements (Gresley's A3, V2 types etc.). The venerable GCR tanks (C13, N5) were still used on local trains and at the Rickmansworth changeover from/to electric traction and for a time the 'Master Cutler' and 'South Yorkshireman' expresses recalled past glories. But yet another review by BR in 1958 led to a transfer of steam operations on the Joint to the Midland Region which, after capitalising on the alternative route offered during the rebuilding of Euston, seized on the opportunity to run down services from Marylebone in favour of its competing route from St Pancras. But soon the service was truncated to just a few semi-fast trains. During this last period, the locomotives employed shifted from ex-LMS engines (Stanier & Fowler tank engines and the ubiquitous class 5s) to the new BR standard steam locomotives (from tank engines to 9Fs and Britannias), which were themselves soon replaced in the 1960s by a fleet of diesel multiple units (Derby 115s) and locomotives for the minimal freight duties. Neasden Shed was closed and the last regular steam-hauled service departed from Marylebone on 3rd September 1966.

In the early 1980s, another BR review of its network strove for profitability by attempting to close Marylebone station and its lines, by diverting the old GW & GC traffic into Paddington, and that of the Met & GC route into Baker Street. The latter route was also under pressure from LT to cut back on the further reaches of the Met at Chesham. The public reaction was far stronger than expected and this pressure revealed that the BR plans and the associated 'Serpell' proposals to convert the old GC tracks into roads were impractical. BR also began to realise that Baker Street and Paddington could not cope with the extra trains and, with their creation of Network South-East under the dynamic Chris Green, there was a U-turn with closure plans withdrawn in 1986. Furthermore, he identified the Birmingham and Aylesbury lines north-west from Marylebone as a suitable case for rejuvenation under the banner of a Thames & Chiltern Division of Network South-East. This modernisation programme of £75 million comprised new trains, a maintenance depot, track, signalling, stations and automatic train protection, giving a major upgrade. The *volte face* was encouragingly completed with the delivery of the new type 165 Turbostar diesel multiple units early in 1992. Indeed, the radical improvement in their services under Adrian Shooter subsequently made the Chiltern Line a prime candidate for privatisation under the Thatcher Government and John Laing backed a successful management buy-out led by Adrian Shooter in 1996 to win a 7-year franchise.

The improved journey times offered by the electrification of the Met to Amersham, and the revitalised Chiltern Railways Turbo service to Aylesbury, almost equalled those achieved in pre-war times and now made the further reaches of Metro-land more feasible for commuting. This was particularly attractive to first-time buyers due to the effect of the lower land prices.

Later, LT were reluctantly swept up in the privatisation move when even the 1997 Labour Government recognised that this was the pragmatic way to obtain the massive investment needed to upgrade the neglected system by means of a Public Private Partnership (PPP). By 2001, LUL had established a number of 'shadow' operating companies, in anticipation of legislation, covering the Sub-Surface Lines (i.e. Met, District, Circle and Hammersmith) and the deep Tube Lines. However, on the election of the maverick Ken Livingstone as the First Mayor of (Greater) London, he established Transport for London (TfL) to integrate London's Transport and fought against the Government's PPP concept. During the consequent delay, the Government came to recognise that Livingstone was popular with Londoners but he eventually had to accept the use of the PPP funding mechanism, as opposed to funding by an issue of bonds. After a complex tendering process, in 2002 a Metronet consortium of W S Atkins, Balfour-Beatty, Bombardier, EDF Energy and Thames Water secured a 30-year lease of all the assets of the Sub Surface Lines (SSL), with the remit to maintain and improve them for operation by LUL. In 2003 LUL formally became part of TfL.

The year 2000 sadly saw the end to a last flourish of a flavour of the Metropolitan Railway, which had begun in 1989 as a celebration of the centenary of the opening of the Chesham Branch. These popular 'Steam on the Met' events enabled vintage steam locomotives to carry passengers over parts of the Extension, recreating the memorable sights and sounds of Metro-land.

ooooo0000ooooo

CHAPTER 15

EPILOGUE

I have rounded off my earlier books on the Joint line with a summary of how the railways of Metro-land were expected to develop in the future. It is therefore somewhat disturbing to realise that, in spite of the expenditure of much time, effort and money over these past 10 years, few of these schemes have yet materialised. Admittedly new railways, especially those through urban areas around London, are inevitably difficult to plan, construct and afford. Unfortunately their realisation also seems incompatible with the political processes which in practice are increasingly constrained by a time horizon of less than the maximum four years of a Government. Even then, those projects that do emerge are emasculated by the annual reviews and consequent uncertainty imposed by the Treasury. In parallel, the current business environment, rightly or wrongly, also requires greater financial transparency and closer adherence to short term targets from the companies undertaking such work. It is probably the case that, in the past, few of our major railways would have been built within the limits of our present financial rules!

Yet another restructuring of rail operations was instituted by the Government in 2004, with the roles of the Strategic Rail Authority and the once independent Rail Regulator being taken back into the Department for Transport (under the aegis of a Director of Railways). At the same time, the infrastructure provider Network Rail (replacing Railtrack) now has no remit to expand the system.

Probably the first of these relevant earlier major schemes was **CrossRail**, born within LT in the 1960s as a deep, 6 m diameter large-bore Tube from Paddington to Liverpool Street. It escalated by the 1990s to a 25 kv overhead electric system, with branches to the west on the Joint via Neasden to Aylesbury, and to Heathrow, as well as Reading. In the east, the line would reach Stratford and Shenfield to create an east-west corridor. Needless to say, the estimated cost and the number of interested parties also increased dramatically, with the Government first using delaying tactics by referring the proposals to the SRA, and then trying to pass responsibility for funding to others. The latest cost estimate is some £3.8 billion just for the tunnel, and it is hoped that finance will come from a combination of the City of London (from an increase in business rates), TfL, and possibly, the Government. In trying to accommodate the wishes of these parties, the objectives have significantly changed. Adrian Montague is now Chairman of Cross London Rail Links and the emphasis is now on the east of London, a strategy which would optimistically support the bid for the 2012 Olympics, also serving the Docklands developments and connecting with the Channel Tunnel Rail Link (CTRL) from St Pancras at Ebbsfleet. However, with this extra expense, the developments to the west of London are now more vague, indeed from the viewpoint of Metro-land, it appears that the route to Aylesbury has now been abandoned. This would mean that the present basic Met and Chiltern line services are not to be truncated as originally envisaged. However, if CrossRail does go ahead, it could indirectly improve all Met services by reducing the growing pressures at the eastern end of the line. The future still remains uncertain, as the enabling hybrid Bill has yet to be passed during the last phase of the current Government, with the earliest possible commencement of construction in about 4 years' time. During this period, more conflicting proposals, like the new 'Superlink' project to extend the catchment area, increase passengers, and thus lower subsidies, could further confuse the situation.

The other impressive project was a private initiative by **Central Railway** in early 1989, echoing Watkin's ideas in that it intended 'to provide increased capacity for freight trains between France via the Channel Tunnel and Liverpool through provision of a dedicated new line, partly formed from the former Great Central route'. As might be expected, those living near the proposed route were incensed and, in spite of intense lobbying by the company, in 2004 the SRA and the Government found insufficient justification for encouragement on financial grounds, in that 'Central Railway's proposal was unlikely to be fundable from the Public purse'. It could also have significantly affected the newly awarded 20-year franchise to Chiltern Railways for part of the route. A further shadow has been cast by the death in 2004 of Andrew Gritten, the main proponent of the scheme.

Unfortunately, two rather more modest improvements to the existing system, which all seemed to agree would be financially viable and useful, are still languishing. The first would be the re-opening and upgrading of the old LMSR line from Bedford and Sandy via Bletchley, Verney Junction, Bicester and Oxford, proposed by the **East-West Consortium** in 1999. This was the pre-war 'Varsity' link between Cambridge and Oxford, which would provide a very useful outer ring serving the East Coast ports and avoiding London. Most of the track remains between Oxford and Bletchley and the SRA has supported a recent upgrade (albeit to a 40 mph maximum!) between Bletchley and Bedford, just leaving the 7-mile gap to Sandy. And although completion of this route could also re-open the possibility of enabling Chiltern Railways to operate north of Aylesbury, the will does not seem to exist to finish this low-cost project.

The other very useful and short connection that has remained in suspended animation for a long time is the **Watford – Croxley Rail Link**, which would divert the Met trains from their present station at Watford to the nearby Watford Junction

With the run-down of steam haulage during the 1960s, DMUs gradually replaced the Marylebone passenger services and diesel locomotives the duties on goods trains. At the top, a class 24 diesel no.D5059 runs round its wagons at Watford station. *(Thomas Scott)* Below, a class 25 no.25306 is passing through Rickmansworth on a proving trip. *(LTM)*

As a precursor to the long-delayed implementation of the pre-war electrification plans in 1961, the signal box at the south end of Rickmansworth station (top) was replaced by a brick LT structure at the north end. The interior of this new box (bottom) shows the extended area of control, encompassing both Watford and the Croxley Tip. *(LTM)*

With electrification, Moor Park underwent a dramatic change. On the left are the remains of the Met up wooden platform and footbridge, where so many waited in the wind, rain and cold to change between slow and fast trains. That on the down side has been replaced by one of the two new LT concrete and brick-style island platforms. *(LTM)*

Looking south from Northwood station during 1960, with the building of the extra tracks in progress for long-delayed improvements to the Met. The original tracks to the right were to become the fast lines shared between the BR/Marylebone and LT/fast services. In the foreground, new slow lines and platforms are being added. *(LTM)*

1960 and the end of the old Chesham Shuttle is nigh, as it climbs out of the Chess Valley through over-arching trees. The track is ready for electrification and the veteran Met Ashbury coaches are now hauled by a BR Ivatt 2-6-2T no.41272, fitted for auto-working. This spot was very exposed and was lined with fences to prevent snow drifting. *(LTM)*

The extra tracks from Harrow and the electrification works to Chesham and Amersham were completed in September 1961, but the new aluminium-built multiple-electric stock were still unready. Thus the old Met T stock continued and the Bo-Bo locos, like 'Sarah Siddons' above, hauled the extended fast trains beyond Rickmansworth.*(LTM)*

Following the 1961 electrification, a number of weak original bridges were replaced and the opportunity taken to widen the roads beneath. Left, a view towards the north end of Rickmansworth station, showing the intense activity to allow the new bridge to be rolled into position. *(WHG)* The scene below at Amersham station marks the end of the distinctive Met Dreadnought coaches, with the last such train alongside a rake of the new A60 multiple electrics. *(S S Gillman)*

By the end of 1961, all of the A60 multiple-electric stock had been delivered and the old Met stock replaced. Here, an impressive number of the A60 sets are lined up, with Neasden power station still dominating the scene. Apart from removal of guard positions and adding end windows, the A60s remain the same over 40 years later. *(Getty Images)*

Even in 1958, although few passenger trains now stopped at Quainton Road station, it still had considerable goods traffic. Looking south towards Aylesbury, on the left the sidings are full of coal wagons whilst on the up line, another coal train with a mixed load is bound for Neasden yard. On the right lies the disused bay platform for Brill. *(BCRO)*

The Midland Region of BR is well represented by two ex-LMS Fairburn 2-6-4 tank engines at the northern end of Aylesbury station in February 1963. On the left, no.42252 on a down stopping train gets the 'right away', whilst in the foreground, the station pilot no.42250 attaches a parcel van to the Marylebone bound up train. *(Tony Newman)*

Harrow at the end of the BR steam era in 1966, with one of the three longer-distance trains left in the daily timetable. A Doncaster-built Riddles standard BR class 5 4-6-0 no.73066 waits as the driver of the pilot engine, a Stanier Type class 5, walks back for a brief word. Then, double-heading was usual to transfer one of the locos. *(H Priestley)*

Even at the end of BR steam services in 1966, LT retained some engines for Met works trains. Between 1956-63, they replaced their venerable Met tank engines with ex-GWR 0-6-0T panniers. Here, one such 57xx engine takes the daily rubbish train from Watford, across Cassio bridge over the Grand Union Canal, to the Croxley tip. *(Les Reason)*

Two pictures of the Chesham branch in the 1950s which encapsulate the charms of Metroland. At the top, the 'Shuttle', with ex-GCR C13 tank engine No.67416 hauling the venerable Ashbury coaches as it curves past Rann's Farm towards Chalfont & Latimer. Here the more adventurous drivers would sometimes race the mainline trains to the station! *(Colin Seabright/Photomatic)*. Below, the passengers alight from the 'Shuttle' that has now arrived at the dedicated bay platform in Chalfont and Latimer station. The driver will now stroll to the cab in the rear coach to use the auto-controls for the return journey. *(LTM)*

mainline station. This would be via a new viaduct about 1 km north of Croxley Green, and the disused Croxley Green-Watford Junction branch over 4.5 km to join the Euston line. Although all parties, including the SRA, have supported such an obviously beneficial scheme, inevitably funding has been the problem. However, the Hertfordshire County Council is now expected to be able to provide about £70 million towards the estimated cost of £90 million, and TfL has brought the project to life by proposing to contribute about £18 million of the rest from recently approved 'discretionary' borrowing. Possibly it might be completed in 2010.

In comparison with this lack of progress, it has been the incumbent Train Operating Companies (TOCs) which have made the significant improvements to rail services in Metro-land. Chiltern Railways, in implementing the plans for their extended 20-year franchise, have achieved the most visible improvements. The upgrades of the old GW & GC route to Birmingham continue, following the reinstatement of double tracking, better stations at Birmingham, and extensions of services to Kidderminster and Stratford. On this, and on the Aylesbury lines, traffic is still increasing at a rate of more than 10% p.a., with one of the best UK punctuality records of 93.3% in 2004. To meet this demand steps are being taken to increase both the infrastructure and the train capacities. At peak times, Marylebone now lacks platform spaces and work has now started on building a new light maintenance depot (originally intended to be on the site of the old LNER loco shed at Neasden, but this conflicted with an earlier route for CrossRail!) near Wembley Stadium station. This will provide for washing, refuelling and basic maintenance to relieve the congestion at Marylebone, giving space to add 2 new platforms in 2006 – as originally intended by GCR! It is also intended to resurrect another GCR intention that was foiled by the Met, namely the construction of a new passenger interchange station at West Hampstead with the Jubilee and Silverlink lines.

These extra services are being operated by completely refurbishing the original type 165 Turbo diesel multiple units and the new more spacious type 168 Clubman DMUs. In addition, the Chiltern Railways main maintenance base at Aylesbury has converted a number of heritage DMUs for use as a Princes Risborough – Aylesbury 'shuttle', and for route learning and track cleaning duties. There has been no progress in extending services much north of Aylesbury, but the single track remains open for the twice-daily refuse train to a landfill site at Calvert, hauled by a massive EWS type 66 General Motors diesel locomotive. But a first step is expected to be the creation of a 'Parkway' station on the north outskirts of Aylesbury to serve the expected expansion of the town.

Progress on the Met line has been caught up in the long-drawn-out political wrangles over control and policy for transport in Greater London, which also has major ramifications for the old Metro-land. The Government imposed the Public

Private Partnership (PPP) approach on the new Mayor, Ken Livingstone, however he is turning the scheme to his own advantage under his Transport for London (TfL). Opinions differ widely on the merits of the PPP arrangement, which now governs how the trains of London Underground are provided for the next 30 years. Basically, the infrastructure and assets of the Sub Surface Lines (SSL) i.e. the Met, District, Circle and Hammersmith lines, have been leased for 30 years to the **Metronet SSL** consortium for maintenance and improvement, whilst still being operated by London Underground, reporting to the American head of TfL, Robert Kiley. Another group, Tubelines, has similar responsibility for the deep level tube lines.

Metronet have inherited a worn infrastructure, with the signalling systems being particularly vulnerable, and the existing A60 multiple electric stock being among some of the oldest operational train sets in the UK. The bogies of the latter have had to be strengthened and the allowed maximum speed reduced from 60 to 50 mph, with a consequent effect on schedules.

Inevitably, there is as yet little to show for Metronet's intentions, but the signs are hopeful. Obviously a lot will depend on the relationship between TfL, LT and Metronet, but it is encouraging that they are tackling fundamentals as well as cosmetic issues. The most basic point that Metronet have revisited is the integration of the various SSLs under their control in terms of trains, control and alternative configuration of the routes, to minimise conflicting movements and give a better overall service. The latter might involve quite radical changes in the routing of existing Circle, Hammersmith and Met services.

New common multiple electric stock is to be introduced to replace the existing Met A stock, District D stock and Hammersmith C stock. It is now expected that the new cars will all be of the shorter 51 ft length, and with a standard seating configuration orientated towards the high density inner London standing pattern, rather than the traditional Met-style layout for longer-distance passengers who expect seating! New features will be air-conditioning and the stock will have end doors enabling passengers to move between cars at all times. The order with Bombardier for 190 sets will comprise 6, 7 and 8 car formations for the SSL fleet, and with solid-state controls, they will have some equipment in common with the complementary new Metronet deep tube stock. To optimise the size of rolling stock, all tunnels are being measured with a trolley-mounted electronic scanner (accurate to 3 mm), to determine clearances relative to track. This is being used in conjunction with tests, which involve lifting and then tilting both empty and fully loaded rolling stock through varying degrees of cant, to measure sway and thus the required clearance.

These new trains are expected to start being delivered in 2009 and are designed to operate up to a maximum speed of 70 mph. They will be fitted with equipment for automatic train operation and also automatic train protection, in conjunction with deployment of a new Westinghouse rolling-block system of signalling throughout the Met. To further improve operations on the Met Extension, a new devolved control centre will be opened at Rickmansworth, and permission will be sought to re-open the old LT tip site at Watford South Junction as a track maintenance base. However, the most visible changes will be the refurbishment and modernisation of some 26 Met stations, including the redevelopment of that serving the new Wembley Stadium complex.

Particular attention is being given to removing the problems associated with the bottle-neck points in London by providing faster turn-rounds and even by extending the existing bay platform 4 at Baker Street station to join the Inner Circle tracks, thus giving trains improved direct access to the City.

The conclusion that could be drawn from the expected progress in the rail travel to Metro-land are more reliable services of higher capacity from both railways. This will involve LT concentrating on the shorter distances and Chiltern Railways tending to reduce the number of stops in that area and running more non-stop trains into Bucks. Perhaps the competitive relationship between the two will produce improvements as the original Joint partnership did?

WHITHER METRO-LAND? These envisaged improvements to the railways will further accelerate the changing face of Metro-land, already influenced by the existing demographic and aspirational trends. This community reflects the national tendencies of more ethnic diversity, an ageing population, and much greater variety with more single people and smaller family units, broken relationships and fewer children. The social and economic consequences of these are profound but, in terms of the impact in our context, it increases the existing pressures on Metro-land with a greater proportion of people wanting their individual home. Understandably, people such as pensioners and the disabled would like more sheltered housing with the availability of appropriate facilities and relevant support. Coupled with the requirements of the single and minimal family units, this creates a growing demand for smaller houses and flats. However, the current boom in the property market is also fuelling the migration of existing home owners to larger properties.

Most people now expect access to facilities, ranging from public services to commercial outlets, with a car to reach them. This creates pressure on roads and, as most hope for at least a parking space at each end of the journey, preferably a garage or safe parking facility for security reasons. Indeed, vulnerability is now a prime concern with more burglar alarms, Neighbourhood Watch groups and interest in 'gated estates' on the lines of American condominiums. A consequence of this defensive attitude is an isolated living style which is becoming more dependent on electronic communication systems such as fixed/mobile telephones, radio/television and the internet, all tending to converge towards an interactive voice, vision and text service.

But these national trends seem unlikely to affect the relative attractions of Metro-land, and thus the demand by people to live there. As London remains an essential location for many organisations, it will also continue to attract an array of supporting commercial, service and retail activities, all with staff who still wish to live in a desirable area. Whereas in the past it was instinctive to use the railways for any travelling (as being cheap, quick, reliable and seemingly door-to-door), nowadays the car is literally just outside, apparently cheap, and can go to the exact destination. Rail travel is often only considered when the road option presents difficulties, such as commuting to towns or the longer inter-city journeys. So, the railways of Metro-land still remain attractive for commuting and accessing the major London termini for onward travel.

Equally, in spite of the weakening of the idealistic concepts of Metro-land under an onslaught of individual housing and commercial developments, the outer reaches do retain something of its rural character. For a short time it will be feasible to create some more housing on in-fill and brown-field sites where developers will probably aim for the desirable smaller properties, like town houses or flats, for better returns. Larger scale development will increasingly be forced further out and will conflict with the growing environmental lobby protecting the inspiration of the Green Belt. However, with the benefit of hindsight it is easy to come to the conclusion that, in the understandable euphoric post-war rush to provide more housing, the opportunity offered by the Abercrombie Plan to optimise our environment was lost.

But equally of concern is the apparent loss of altruistic planning and development at a local level that could result in a more harmonious environment. In practice, it seems as if much new development is considered on a very narrow basis due to small parcels of land becoming available or requests for the insidious 'change of use'. The process itself works against quality, where proposals are judged within a complex of committee systems, and the inevitable result is the lowest common factor rather than the highest common denominator – as in the saying that a camel is a horse designed by a committee! This is not to claim that a more directed approach is necessarily the answer, but surely we could do better than the current ad hoc building developments driven by specific, unrelated, commercial developments.

There is no doubt that those who currently live in Metro-land can point to many changes for the worse but, on the positive side, I suggest that looking back to the beginnings of Watkin's railway, these are less than might be expected. Certainly, there are the downsides of modern trends in affluence, congestion, pollution, communications etc., where we are still seeking to strike the right balance. But even considering these factors, Watkin might think that Metro-land has survived remarkably well. It still offers wide open spaces looking across to Harrow-on-the-Hill, the 'new' houses at Moor Park hidden in the trees, Rickmansworth with its lakes and park, Chorleywood with its Common, and then the ride on the Chesham branch under overarching trees down to the River Chess *(see below, Chesham station in 1957 – CfBS)*. The main line itself still climbs over the largely unspoilt beeches of the Chilterns and down to the Vale of Aylesbury.

Probably some came to this book wondering if the attractions of Metro-land ever existed beyond the blinkered eyes of the beholders, or in the imaginative publicity of the Met. I hope that I have convinced them of a reality in the charm of the Metropolitan Railway and the area it served. Whilst the railway was heralded as bringing more freedom, it also propagated a sense of cohesion and social order. In practice, most of the residents of Metro-land found it a pleasant place to live in, and with the services provided by London Transport via the Met and the range of familiar red and green buses, they had the nearest yet we seem to have reached towards an integrated transport system.

"Then visualise, far down the shining lines,
 Your parents' homestead set in murmuring pines." – John Betjeman

REFERENCES

As this book is to an extent complementary my the two previous books about the Joint, the references shown below are *additional* to those quoted in the earlier books. However, it is first appropriate to highlight that the key basic sources are:

Dow, George	*The Great Central Railway*, Vols. 1-3		
		Locomotive Pub. Co.	1959
Goudie, Frank	*Metropolitan Steam Locomotives*		
		Capital Transport	1990
Greaves, Canon John	*Sir Edward Watkin*		
		The Book Guild	2005
Jackson, Alan A	*London's Metropolitan Railway*		
		David and Charles	1986
Barman, Christian	*The Man who Built London Transport*		
		David and Charles	1979

Also, the primary Metropolitan Railway and Met & GC Joint Committee records are held at The London Metropolitan Archive, under Accession No. 1297.

Additional Sources

Abercrombie, Patrick	*The Greater London Plan*	1944
	HMSO	
Goudie, Frank	*Baker Street Station*	1992/3
	Railways South-East, Vol.3 p.168	
Halliday, Stephen	*Underground To Everywhere*	2002
	Sutton	
McDermott, F	*The Life And Work of Joseph Firbank*	1887
	Longmans, Green	
Rolt, L T C	*George and Robert Stephenson*	1960
	Longmans	
Simmons, Jack	*Companion to British Railway History*	1997
	Oxford	
White, H P	*Regional History of Railways of Great Britain*	
	Vol.3	1987
	David and Charles	

ooooo00000ooo